"This book is the best th.... that the parallels drawn by ..... Adam) necessitate viewing not only Christ as a historical figure but also the first Adam as an actual historical figure. The argument is made persuasively and convincingly that, if one concludes that the first Adam was not historical, then one should be driven to the conclusion that Jesus as the Last Adam was not historical—the latter conclusion even very few unbelieving scholars would be willing to hold. Other references to Adam outside of Paul in the New Testament are also discussed, and the same conclusion is convincingly reached about the historicity of the first Adam. One might not agree with everything said about other issues outside of the Adam-Christ topic, but the conclusions reached about Adam and Christ are sane, sober, and reliable."

—**Gregory K. Beale,** Professor of New Testament and Biblical Theology, Westminster Theiological Seminary

"Many thanks for reissuing this helpful work. Among its many virtues let me mention two. First, Versteeg stresses clearly that Paul's arguments in Romans and 1 Corinthians depend on historical sequence: Adam did something, and as a result something happened, and then Jesus came to deal with the consequences of it all. In this process both Adam and Jesus acted as representatives. Second, our view of Adam is bound up with our view of sin: is it an intruder into God's good world (the traditional position), or is it a necessary part of the creation (which denial of historical Adam entails)? Anyone reading this will appreciate that contemporary discussions of Adam are still treading the same ground."

—**C. John Collins,** Professor of Old Testament, Covenant Theological Seminary

"Denying the historicity of Adam or his significance for our own original sin is not just an issue of science versus the Old Testament. For the New Testament, as in Romans 5, deals with Adam as well, in an important theological context. For the apostle Paul, our sin begins in Adam, as our redemption begins in Christ. Theologians cannot escape this teaching merely by saying that Adam is a myth or legend; they must also account for his role in Paul's doctrine of salvation. So a number of theologians, such as H. M. Kuitert, have postulated that Adam is a 'teaching model' in the New Testament. Versteeg's remarkably cogent and concise book tells us why this view is impossible. It was a great help to us when it was first published in 1979. But it is even more helpful now. Recently, some have claimed that analysis of the human genome forbids us to believe that the human race began with a single couple. In the face of such arguments, it is important to remind ourselves why the church has maintained that Adam is the first man and the source of human sin. I do hope this book gets a wide readership."

—**John M. Frame,** Professor of Systematic Theology and Philosophy, Reformed Theological Seminary, Orlando

"Given the recent debates about the existence of Adam, this vigorous defense of historical Adam is as relevant now as it was when first published in Dutch. The exegetical and theological issues remain the same today. Versteeg shows with vigor and cogency that the New Testament's teaching requires a historical Adam, and his defense deserves the attention of all who are interested in the question."

—**Vern S. Poythress,** Professor of New Testament Interpretation and Editor of the *Westminster Theological Journal,* Westminster Theological Seminary

"What an important book this is for today! Sane, clear and thorough, it offers a stout answer for those questioning the historicity of Adam, and lucidly shows why it remains non-negotiable. All thinking Christians need to read this."

—**Michael Reeves,** Head of Theology, University and Colleges Christian Fellowship

Adam in the
New Testament

Adam in the New Testament

MERE TEACHING MODEL OR
FIRST HISTORICAL MAN?

SECOND EDITION

J. P. Versteeg

Translated by Richard B. Gaffin Jr.

P&R
PUBLISHING
P.O. BOX 817 • PHILLIPSBURG • NEW JERSEY 08865-0817

This book is a slightly abridged translation of the chapter titled "Is Adam in het Nieuwe Testament een 'leermodel'?," *Woord en Kerk: Theologische bijdragen van de hoogleraren aan de Theologische Hogeschool der Christelijke Gereformeerde Kerken in Nederland bij de herdenking van het vijfenzeventigjarig bestaan van de Hogeschool* (Amsterdam: T. Bolland, 1969), 29–70. It was previously published in 1978 as *Is Adam a "Teaching Model" in the New Testament? An Examination of One of the Central Points in the Views of H. M. Kuitert and Others* by Presbyterian and Reformed Publishing Company, Nutley, NJ.

ISBN: 978-1-59638-522-1 (pbk)
ISBN: 978-1-59638-581-8 (ePub)
ISBN: 978-1-59638-582-5 (Mobi)

Printed in the United States of America

Library of Congress Cataloging-in-Publication Data

Versteeg, J. P.
   [Is Adam in het Nieuwe Testament een "leermodel"? English]
   Adam in the New Testament : mere teaching model or first historical man? / J.P. Versteeg ; translated by Richard B. Gaffin, Jr. -- 2nd ed.
       p. cm.
   Includes bibliographical references.
   ISBN 978-1-59638-522-1 (pbk.)
   1. Adam (Biblical figure) I. Title.
   BS580.A4V4813 2012
   222'.11092--dc23
                                2012025653

CONTENTS

Preface to the
1978 Edition

ONE QUESTION at the center of interest throughout the world is that of the origin and essence of man. From where does man come and who is he? When we take up this question in the light of Scripture, we immediately encounter what Scripture says about Adam. However, what is the intention of Scripture when it speaks about Adam? Does Scripture characterize Adam as a historical person in whom the history of humanity began, or merely as a model, used in a framework of teaching—as a "teaching model"—without historical significance? The answer to this question has far-reaching consequences. One's view of sin, redemption, and the Redeemer is closely connected with one's view of Adam.

This study, which will examine what Scripture says about Adam, was originally a contribution to a volume published for the 75th anniversary of the Theological Seminary of the Christian Reformed Churches in the Netherlands and written by the professors of the seminary. It was intended as a New Testament contribution to that volume. For this reason attention has been limited to the data of the New Testament.

My thanks to the translator for his readiness to make this study available in English.

J. P. Versteeg (1938–87)

TRANSLATOR'S FOREWORD

FOR THIS REPRINTING, the translation has been slightly modified in a few places but remains substantially unchanged. Works cited in the footnotes have been updated with their English translations appearing since 1978, with the exception of G. C. Berkouwer's two-volume work on Scripture, whose single-volume English translation has been so substantially edited as to preclude accurate reference to the latter in Versteeg's citations.

When this work appeared over forty years ago, I was drawn to making it available in English for its effective refutation of the view that Scripture does not require the historic Christian confession that all human beings descend from Adam as the first human being. Also, its careful and incisive examination of key New Testament passages makes an important positive contribution in its own right.

Versteeg, since deceased, dealt primarily with the views of H. M. Kuitert as well as of several others gaining currency at that time within Protestant and Roman Catholic circles in the Netherlands. Little did I imagine then the way in which virtually the same views have subsequently become increasingly present within English-speaking evangelical circles on both sides of the Atlantic. This is true particularly for a number of scientists, biblical scholars, and others who believe, moreover, that their denial or, as the case may be, doubts about the historic Christian understanding of Adam and his significance should be accepted as compatible with their Christian commitment.

Versteeg challenges that conviction. He shows that it conflicts with the central message of Scripture and leads to the eventual loss of the gospel. This is the basic thread of his argumentation: if it is not true that all human beings descend from Adam as the first human being, then the entire history of redemption documented in Scripture unravels. The result is no redemptive *history* in any credible or coherent sense and so the loss of *redemptive* history in any meaningful sense.

Versteeg's work is as timely today as when it was first written. The publisher is to be commended for making its translation available again.[1]

In his concluding chapter (6), Versteeg notes some primary "Consequences" of embracing an evolutionary view of human origins and denying the historicity of Adam as affirmed and reflected on in Scripture. He identifies three such far-reaching implica-

1. Among more recent brief treatments of the biblical and theological issues at stake, see Michael Reeves, "Adam and Eve," in *Should Christians Embrace Evolution? Biblical and Scientific Responses*, ed. Norman C. Evans (Phillipsburg, NJ: P&R Publishing, 2009), 43–56; Robert B. Strimple, "Was Adam Historical?" in *Confident of Better Things: Essays Commemorating Seventy-five Years of the Orthodox Presbyterian Church*, ed. John R. Muether and Danny E. Olinger (Willow Grove, PA: Committee for the Historian of the Orthodox Presbyterian Church, 2011), 215–22; Richard B. Gaffin Jr., "'All Mankind Descending from Him . . .'?," *New Horizons* 33, 3 (March 2012): 3–5.

tions for the Christian faith. The most immediate is a radically altered understanding of *sin*, particularly of the origin and nature of human depravity and the corresponding abandonment of any meaningful notion of the *guilt* of sin. This changed view of sin, in turn, results in a substantially changed notion of *salvation*. Eclipsed or even denied is Christ's death as a substitutionary atonement that propitiates God's just and holy wrath on sin and removes its guilt. And these shifted perceptions of sin and salvation are inevitably followed by a significantly different assessment of the *Savior*. Stressed is Christ's humanity, especially the exemplary aspects of his person and work (he is the "ideal man" realized within the constraints of the evolutionary process), an emphasis that minimizes or even denies his deity.

Versteeg details these consequences as he encountered them. It is worth taking some note here how they—particularly those concerning sin and salvation—are finding expression today among the group mentioned above: would-be evangelicals who hold that denying the historicity of Adam as taught in the Bible is nonetheless compatible with Christianity true to the Bible. One such instance is the recent book of Peter Enns.[2]

Enns writes primarily for those like him who want to remain Christians faithful to Scripture yet also share his conviction that scientific evidence renders no longer credible the historic Christian confession "all mankind, descending from him [Adam] by ordinary generation, sinned in him, and fell with him, in his first transgression."[3] The evidence, he believes, is beyond dispute

2. *The Evolution of Adam: What the Bible Does and Doesn't Say about Human Origins* (Grand Rapids: Brazos, 2012).
3. Westminster Shorter Catechism 16; Westminster Larger Catechism 22.

that human beings have evolved from earlier forms of life and by a process that excludes the possibility that all human beings descended from an original first pair. This conviction has led to his book and controls from beginning to end his effort to show that a divinely facilitated ("theistic") macro-evolutionary view of the origin of the universe in general and of humanity in particular is compatible with how Scripture is to be read and is normative today.

The scientific issues involved, certainly important and in need of careful attention, are not my concern here. Nor for the most part is Enns' handling of Scripture (his treatment of Paul's teaching on Adam, which he clearly recognizes provides the greatest obstacle for the compatibility view that he wishes to establish, is akin to the views that Versteeg addresses and refutes). My interest, rather, is the theological conclusions and implications for the Christian faith that he is brought to by his controlling conviction that the findings of evolutionary science must be determinative for understanding the Bible and its authority today. Enns and others who share this conviction may not explicitly draw particular conclusions or implications and may even wish not to do so. But it is difficult at best to see how they can evade them or have other alternatives, at least credible or satisfactory ones.

"*A true rapprochement between evolution and Christianity requires a synthesis, not simply adding evolution to existing theological formulations.*"[4] This, the last of nine concluding theses, is the note on which the book ends. We are not left in any doubt about its implications for the existing theological formulations

4. Enns, *Evolution of Adam*, 147 (italics original).

of historic Christianity, especially as they are found in Reformation and post-Reformation Protestant orthodoxy. The "synthesis" or rethinking that Enns envisions means their complete abandonment.

Evolution, Enns says, has "turned on its head" the Bible's, especially Paul's, teaching about the origin and nature of humanity, sin, and death.[5] Evolution leaves no place for an original state of affairs as described in Genesis 1–2—one, all told, that was "very good" (1:31) and unmarred by the presence and effects of sin. There never was a time when man, created male and female in God's image, lived in undisturbed fellowship with God and each other without sinning and without yet being invariably disposed to sinning. Nor is human death "the unnatural state introduced by a disobedient couple in a primordial garden."[6]

Concerning sin, then, Enns and others of like mind today make clear what is also true of those whom Versteeg dealt with in his day. Evolution excludes believing the Bible's claim that sin entered human history at a point after its beginning. Evolution, in other words, precludes the fall as taught in Scripture. It replaces the historical before-and-after of creation and fall with their side-by-side inseparability. Sin is not a matter of human *fallenness* but of human *givenness*. Whatever else being human may mean, it entails being sinful, or at least being naturally and inalterably disposed to sin.

Enns adopts a "crucial theological distinction" from an article by George L. Murphy, the distinction between "original sin" and

5. Ibid.
6. Ibid.

"sin of origin."[7] The former is the Augustinian notion, alleged to be no longer viable either historically or theologically. "The latter affirms the absolute inevitability of sin that affects every human being from *their* beginnings, from birth." The "self-evident reality of repeated, relentless sin remains an unalterable and existential fact of human existence."[8]

On the same page, Enns is eloquent about this self-evident reality or "what the Judeo-Christian tradition calls sin." But eloquent as well is his complete silence about the *guilt* of sin. The exclusive focus of his description is on sin as the harmful and manipulative things that people do to each other and themselves; all told, they "find it tremendously difficult to live in true peace with each other," and "few are at peace even with themselves."[9]

Not only is there this silence about the guilt that sin incurs (true as well in those whom Versteeg deals with), but also there is no mention or even intimation that sin is rebellion *against God*. Missing is even the slightest indication that the deepest dimension of sin is not the wrongs we do to other people or ourselves, no matter how horrendous, but our personal affront to God in his holiness and sinless purity. "We have all fallen short of the mark," Enns says. But nothing is said about what constitutes and determines this mark, other than that we "see how distant we are from the human ideal that Jesus models."[10]

7. Ibid., 124; the distinction is elaborated on page 111 (see 117n16) in Murphy's "Roads to Paradise and Perdition: Christ, Evolution and Original Sin," *Perspectives on Science and Christian Faith* 58, 2 (June 2006): 109–18.

8. Enns, *Evolution of Adam*, 124 (italics original).

9. One wonders how in Enns' view *any* have a capacity for true peace, whether with themselves or others.

10. Ibid.

Enns' evolution-determined view of sin may have room for some notion of guilt. But it is difficult to see how that will be anything more than guilt in terms of intrahuman relationships and the violation of standards ultimately set by human beings in seeking to maintain and secure some measure of viable communal order and "domestic tranquility" in the face of an inherently destabilizing evolutionary process. It is hardly guilt *coram Deo* in any credible sense.

Enns says that "we must remain open on the ultimate origins of *why* all humans are born in sin (original sin)" and be content with observing "*that* all humans are born in sin (sin of origin)."[11] But this is said in the face of his own unquestioning commitment to a theory that unavoidably entails its own ultimate explanation why all human beings are born in sin. That explanation is, in a word, God. If God, insofar as he is affirmed as in some sense Creator, has set in motion and sustained the evolutionary process so that an eventual outcome is human beings with an inborn disposition to sin, then accountability for that disposition is his, not theirs. This conclusion is inescapable—unless we diminish either the nature of sin or the sovereignty of God as Creator taught in Scripture.[12]

Enns tells us that "characteristics that Christians have thought of as sinful," such as "the aggression and dominance associated with 'survival of the fittest' and sexual promiscuity

11. Ibid., 125 (italics original).
12. This divine accountability is far removed from Reformed theology's view that sin and the fall are comprehended within God's all-controlling eternal decree. That Adam and Eve were created, as they in fact were, able to sin (*posse peccare*) as well as able not to sin (*posse non peccare*) is antithetical to the view that they were created inherently disposed to sin and incapable of not sinning (*non posse non peccare*).

to perpetuate one's gene pool," are evolutionary "means of ensuring survival."[13] If that is so, then no amount of emphasizing the responsibility or the presumed freedom to curb these and other similar inborn proclivities for our own and others' welfare will be able to veil the fact that these proclivities as such are hardly guilt-incurring. They are aspects, givens, of who we are as human beings, essential to what God has used evolution to make us to be. Nor can we be held guilty for their destructive expressions in more than the most relative and attenuated sense. Certainly, guilt before God, even if it were to be affirmed, has been rendered virtually meaningless.

Concerning salvation, Enns repeatedly assures his primary evangelical target audience that the evangel, the gospel, "does not hang in the balance" in his evolution-determined treatment of the Bible's teaching on Adam. He is emphatic: rejecting Paul's teaching about the historicity of Adam "has no bearing whatsoever on the truth of the gospel." Again, he is sure that "the need for a savior does not require a historical Adam."[14]

If we ask, however, what for Enns the gospel confidently deemed not to be at stake is, the answer is anything but adequate. He says repeatedly that the gospel, especially for Paul, is about the death and resurrection of Christ.[15] But he does not say what it is about these events that makes them the core of the gospel nor give any indication how they accomplish salvation from sin and its consequences. There is not even a brief explanation, which his readers might reasonably expect, why, for instance, it is "of first

13. Ibid., 147.
14. Ibid., xix, 102, 143; see other similar statements, 92, 95, 123, passim.
15. Ibid., 123, 131, 143, passim.

importance" in the gospel Paul preached that "Christ died for our sins in accordance with the Scriptures," and therefore "that he was raised on the third day in accordance with the Scriptures" (1 Cor. 15:3–4), or what it means that he "was delivered up for our trespasses and raised for our justification" (Rom. 4:25), to quote another New Testament gospel summary.

Enns is silent about how Christ's death functions for the salvation of sinners—a silence to which he is hardly entitled, given his assertion that the cross is at the heart of the gospel that he is concerned to assure his readers is not put in jeopardy by his views on Adam and sin. Unsurprisingly in light of what has already been noted about his view of sin, there is no mention of the death of Christ as God's unparalleled display of his great love for guilty sinners. It does not enter the picture for him that the cross manifests the depths of God's mercy in establishing permanent peace and reconciliation with sinners by propitiating his just and holy wrath against their sin and so removing the guilt that their sin incurs. It is difficult to see what place, if any, Enns sees for the penal substitutionary aspect of the atonement taught in Scripture. Beyond its exemplary aspect, Christ's death appears to be no more than the necessary precondition for his resurrection as the event that overcomes the power of sin and death.[16]

16. The issue here is not: either penal substitution or *Christus Victor*. Both views of the atonement are true. But the latter, properly understood, is true only because of the former. There is no deliverance from sin's power and enslaving corruption (sanctification) without freedom from its guilt (justification). As it has been put rather pungently recently, "Sorry, but victory without the penal is pyrrhic." Robert H. Gundry, "Smithereens!" review of *The Bible Made Impossible: Why Biblicism Is Not a Truly Evangelical Reading of Scripture*, by Christian Smith, http://www.booksand culture.com/articles/2011/sepoct/smithreens.html, para. 12.

For Enns, the permanent truth of the Christian gospel, the enduring good news for today, is the resurrection of Jesus. Unlike Adam as the first to sin, he considers the resurrection a historical event. This resurrection-focus, however, raises a number of questions and prompts the following observations. At best unclear, despite his affirmation of its historicity, is the reality and significance of the resurrection—whether for Jesus himself or for Christians, both for their present experience and as their future hope.

Without arguing in detail here, the New Testament teaches that both the resurrection of Christ and the future resurrection of Christians at his return is bodily (e.g., 1 Cor. 15:12–23). With all the attendant mystery and discontinuity undoubtedly involved, there is underlying continuity, bodily continuity. Their future resurrection bodies will be the outcome of the transformation by the Holy Spirit of their present psychophysical existence. The magnitude of this Spirit-worked change will be such that they will be permanently freed from sin and death along with all the other ravages of sin, a freedom in which the entire creation will share (e.g., Rom. 8:19–22; 1 Cor. 15:42–54; Phil. 3:21).[17] In other words, with all the mystery and whatever more may be involved, the resurrection includes an inalienable biological aspect: the removal of biological death.

It is difficult to see how the evolutionary understanding of human beings and their origin embraced by Enns and others can accommodate this biblical, Pauline understanding of res-

17. Geerhardus Vos, *The Pauline Eschatology* (1930; repr., Grand Rapids: Baker, 1979), 206–14, remains one of the best treatments of this bodily change to be experienced by Christians.

urrection. Evolution has no place for human existence without biological death.

For Enns and others of like mind, then, Paul is quite wrong when he says, with bodily, biological death surely included, that "the wages of sin is death" (Rom. 6:23). And if Paul is wrong about that, then he is equally wrong in teaching, as he clearly does in Romans 4:25 and 1 Corinthians 15:3–4, 17, for instance, that bodily resurrection is an essential and climactic aspect of salvation from sin. In other words, if Paul is wrong about bodily death as a consequence of sin, then he is seriously in error about the *gospel*. Enns' assurances notwithstanding, the gospel does in fact stand or fall with the Bible's teaching on the origin, nature, and consequences of human sin, as that teaching depends upon the historicity of Adam and his fall into sin.

Evolution excludes biblical teaching on "last things" no less than on "first things." The two, as we will presently note further, are inextricably tethered to each other. The Bible's eschatology is no more compatible with evolution than its protology.

For Enns, the present validity and relevance of the gospel appears to center specifically on the "experience of the risen Jesus" had by Paul (and presumably other New Testament writers, though he mentions only Paul).[18] That experience Enns sees as the heart of what the gospel has to offer people today, an experience that possesses enduring reality, he reasons, because Jesus' resurrection was a historical event in the recent past for Paul. His witness to its historicity and to his experience rooted

18. Enns, *Evolution of Adam*, 135, 142.

in it therefore has credibility, unlike his belief in the historicity of Adam in the distant primordial past.[19]

Paul's experience of the resurrected Christ can hardly be construed in this fashion. What we know about his experience comes from what he says about it. That happens as notably as anywhere else in Philippians 3:10–11, "that I may know him and the power of his resurrection, and may share his sufferings, becoming like him in his death, that by any means possible I may attain the resurrection from the dead." Here, autobiographically but representatively for all Christians, Paul expresses his deep aspiration for a full, experiential knowledge of Christ.[20] That knowledge, he says, consists in his present union[21] with the resurrected Christ, marked by the fellowship of suffering and cross-conformity that this union entails. At the same time, this present resurrection experience is oriented to the future, to the resurrection of the body at Christ's return (see also vv. 20–21).

Elsewhere, Paul expands on the future experience of resurrection not just as it will be for him, but for all Christians. "As was the earthly man, so also are those who are earthly, and as is the heavenly man, so also are those who are heavenly. And just as we have borne the image of the earthly man, we shall also bear the image of the heavenly man" (1 Cor. 15:48–49).[22] "The earthly man" is "the first man Adam" (v. 45), and in relation to Adam as the first human being, Christ, "the heavenly man," is "the second man," "the last Adam" (vv. 47, 45).

19. Ibid., 125–26.
20. Summed up as "the surpassing worth of knowing Christ Jesus my Lord" (v. 8).
21. "That I may gain Christ and be found in him" (vv. 8–9).
22. My translation; "heavenly" here describes the resurrected Christ as ascended.

Within the comprehensive outlook of the immediate context (1 Cor. 15:42–49), spanning as it does the whole of human history from its beginning to its consummation, no one else but Adam and Christ comes into consideration; no one else "counts." In their representative and determinative roles, there is no one before Adam, no one between Adam and Christ, and no one after Christ. Christ, in his person and work, is "second" and "last" in relation to Adam as "first." Furthermore, Adam is "first" in relation to those who "bear [his] image." Adam is in view here in solidarity with all other human beings, who, by descending from him, are in natural image-bearing union with him.

Verse 49 is clear. Christians will bear with Christ the "heavenly" image that is now his, the image of God redeemed and glorified by his death, resurrection, and ascension—but only as they have borne Adam's "earthly" image, the original image of God defaced by sin and its consequences. It is quite foreign to this passage, especially given its comprehensive outlook, to suppose that some not in the image of Adam as the first human being will bear the image of the exalted Christ. There is no hope of salvation for sinners who do not bear the image of Adam by ordinary generation. Christ does not and cannot redeem what he has not assumed, and what he has assumed is the human nature of those who bear the image of Adam by natural descent.[23]

23. Enns is sure that in Genesis 1–2 the image of God is no more than functional: it does not refer to a "quality that separates humans from animals" but to "humanity's role of ruling God's creation as God's representative." Enns, *Evolution of Adam*, xv. Yet as Paul understands Genesis 2:7 in its context with its implications (1 Cor. 15:45–49) and as Scripture as a whole teaches, the image of God is above all the body-soul, psychophysical personal being that man, male and female, in distinction from all other animate beings, primate or other, *is*. Biblical anthropology excludes a purely functional view of the divine image. In distinguishing as Scripture does

This passage has in view full, bodily bearing of the image of the resurrected Christ in the future. Elsewhere, Paul is clear that for believers the experience of being conformed to Christ's glory-image is already underway (2 Cor. 3:18; 4:6; cf. 4:16). Present experience of the risen Christ consists in this ongoing conformity "from one degree of glory to another," but only as that experience will culminate in the future resurrection-glorification of the body. Essential to Paul's present "experience of the risen Jesus," then, is his envisioning its consummation in the future in his own resurrected body. There is no place for the former experience without the eventual realization of the latter.

Enns does not discuss the future bodily resurrection. But it is difficult to see, as already noted, how he could find Paul's teaching credible and still relevant today. Furthermore, the difficulty here is in seeing how his evolution-determined approach to the text would leave him with any good reason for not viewing that teaching as couched in the imaginative, speculatively colored apocalyptic outlook present in Second Temple Judaism. This apocalypticism, too, like assumptions about an original first man, is expressed "in the biblical idiom available to him."[24] Since that is the case, the one is no more valid today than the other. Whatever else it may be, Enns' evolution-conditioned "experience of the risen Jesus" is not Paul's.

---

between ontology or being (who man as God's image is) and function (what man as God's image is to do), the former is antecedent to the latter and the latter unintelligible apart from the former. As far as I can see, evolution-determined approaches to Scripture, such as that of Enns, are hard-pressed to come to terms with the body as a constitutive element of the *imago Dei*, a truth that the resurrection of the body, as taught in this passage for one, makes clear.

24. Enns, *Evolution of Adam*, 142.

With all the differences there undoubtedly are, it is difficult to evade the conclusion that Enns' assessment of Paul, like the assessments dealt with by Versteeg, is akin to the view perhaps most clearly articulated in late-nineteenth and early-twentieth-century Older Liberal treatment of Paul with its categorical disjunction between the religion of Paul and the theology of Paul. The former is what is essential: the enduring, perennially valid core of religious conviction and experience to be freed from its outer shell marked by theological dissonance and misconception.[25] Pertinent in this regard is Ned Stonehouse's perceptive observation about the positive understanding of contemporary Christianity that invariably results from the conclusions reached by the historical-critical approach to the Bible. He speaks of "what may with very little exaggeration be characterized as the persistence of Liberalism."[26]

Finally, not to be missed is the view of Scripture involved in making contemporary evolutionary theory decisive for interpreting Scripture and for deciding what in it is or is not valid and relevant today. Enns effectively denies the divine authorship and commensurate authority of the Bible according to its own self-witness. This happens largely through his misuse of the analogy between Christ's incarnation and Scripture.[27] On his

25. On this Liberal view, see Herman Ridderbos, *Paul: An Outline of His Theology*, trans. John Richard De Witt (Grand Rapids: Eerdmans, 1975), 17–22.

26. Ned B. Stonehouse, *Origins of the Synoptic Gospels: Some Basic Questions* (Grand Rapids: Eerdmans, 1963), 154 (with an eye to mid-twentieth-century developments).

27. Enns, *Evolution of Adam*, xi–xii, 143–45. Enns' lengthy quote (144) from Herman Bavinck to support his use of this analogy is specious to an extreme. It would be difficult to find a more misleading understatement when he adds, "By citing Bavinck, I do not mean to suggest that he would apply this principle precisely as I do to this same issue" (161n3). In fact, in applying the "principle" (the incarnational analogy) to the "issue" involved, Bavinck reaches conclusions that could

construal of this analogy, Scripture as a whole embodies God's accommodation to the point where divine authorship, if he still wishes to affirm it in some sense, is no more than a function of human authorship, rather than the reverse.[28] Divine authorship is reduced to the questionable efforts of the human authors—to texts decisively determined, in content as well as form, by their personal limitations and their inadequate and now-outdated cultural assumptions and outlooks, including their errors, even massive errors, both historical and theological, such as Paul's on Adam. On Enns' understanding of divine accommodation and the incarnational analogy, the Bible's divine authorship, that it is ultimately *God's* Word, his *written* Word, has been effectively abandoned in any meaningful sense.

The words with which Versteeg ends his study sound a still-timely warning—appropriate, too, for concluding this Foreword:

> As the first historical man and head of humanity, Adam is not mentioned merely in passing in the New Testament. The redemptive-historical correlation between Adam and Christ determines the framework in which—particularly for Paul—the redemptive work of Christ has its place. That

---

hardly be more diametrically opposed to those of Enns—basic conclusions about Scripture that Enns rejects. See Richard B. Gaffin Jr., *God's Word in Servant-Form: Abraham Kuyper and Herman Bavinck on the Doctrine of Scripture* (Jackson, MS: Reformed Academic Press, 2008), 4–5, 47–107; on the passage Enns cites in its immediate context, 76–79.

28. Repeatedly, without exception as far as I can see, Enns characterizes all the Old and New Testament documents, particularly Genesis and the rest of the Pentateuch, as having no higher authorial origin, as texts, than that they are various reflexive efforts, dubious at numerous points, at "*self*-definition," as Israel's or the church's "*self*-defining" statements. Enns, *Evolution of Adam*, xviii, 6, 32–34, 59, 65, 73, 141 (italics added).

work of redemption can no longer be confessed according to the meaning of Scripture, if it is divorced from the framework in which it stands there. Whoever divorces the work of redemption from the framework in which it stands in Scripture no longer allows the Word to function as the norm that determines *everything*. There has been no temptation down through the centuries that theology has been more exposed to than this temptation. There is no danger that theology has more to fear than this danger.

Richard B. Gaffin Jr.
June 2012

1

THE CONCEPT "TEACHING MODEL"

THE WAY the Bible speaks about Adam is under vigorous discussion today. That way of speaking is often characterized as a "teaching model," a notion found in the booklet of H. M. Kuitert, *Do You Understand What You Read?*

For Kuitert, the all-important consideration is that we see the biblical writers within the framework of their own time. "The time-bound dimension of Scripture," he says, "is . . . essential to its very character." Important questions for understanding Scripture have a direct relation to this "time-boundedness." Kuitert points, for example, to the fact that the biblical writer can speak of a "firmament" that God has created (Gen. 1:6 KJV), while we know that one cannot speak of a firmament in a literal sense. The blue expanse above our heads is not an outspread blue cloth or something of that sort but an effect of light. In the same context, Adam and Eve are mentioned. Just as we find little to indicate that the "firmament" really exists in the sense of something spread out above us, so we find little evidence—the farther we go back in history—for a first set of parents in a garden of Eden. "On the contrary, the oldest humanity for which we have evidence appears to be of a very primitive sort, hardly like the neatly portrayed Adam of Genesis." Therefore Kuitert has "as little difficulty" with the existence of Adam and Eve as with the existence of the firmament. "The living world in which the writer of Genesis expresses himself as he proclaims God as the creator was a world in which a first married couple was as much a natural part as was a firmament. Both elements fit the picture people had of the world at that time. When we confess today that God is the creator, we do that with the help of our current scientific knowledge and thus we speak about evolution, cells, and atoms."[1]

The way the New Testament speaks about Adam does not force Kuitert to revise this conclusion. That would be necessary if we had to understand what the New Testament says about Adam, especially what Paul says in Romans 5, in the sense it was usually taken in earlier times, namely, as decisive for the question concerning the historicity of Adam. According to Kuitert, however, modern biblical study has made clear that the question about the historicity of Adam does not come within the purview of the New Testament, not even Romans 5. When in Romans 5 a parallel is drawn between Adam and Christ, that happens only for the purpose "of illuminating through Adam the meaning and scope of Jesus Christ and his

1. H. M. Kuitert, *Do You Understand What You Read?*, trans. L. Smedes (Grand Rapids, 1970), 36–37.

work. Adam serves Paul by helping the apostle preach Jesus."[2] Because of this specific connection in which Romans 5 speaks of Adam, namely, in the interests of instruction about Christ, the historical aspect we wish to retain for Adam could be considerably less conclusive for Paul than for us. Then follow the words in which the term "teaching model" occurs: "As a pedagogical example or, if you will, a teaching model, Adam does not have to be a historical figure."[3] In order to avoid any misunderstanding, Kuitert has explicitly assured us that the historical aspect of Adam was far less important for Paul than for us. He derives this from the fact that in Romans 5:12–21 it is essential to Paul's argument that Adam and not Eve was the first transgressor, while in 1 Timothy 2:14 the reverse is the case. There Paul argues that Eve, not Adam, began to sin. According to Kuitert, the one instance in the nature of the case excludes the other and proves that Paul was not interested in the historical course of things. As a student of the rabbis, Paul used all sorts of Scripture passages for his own purpose, and that purpose was to make clear the significance of Jesus as the Messiah. Paul was concerned with Adam not as a historical figure but only as an instructional or teaching model.[4]

It is not clear from whom Kuitert borrows the term "teaching model," granted that he borrows it and that it is not his own invention. His use of the term displays an obvious similarity to the use of the term "model" by C. A. Van Peursen in his *Filosofische orientatie*. In this study the concept "model,"

2. Ibid., 40.
3. Ibid.
4. Ibid., 40–41.

borrowed by Van Peursen from the natural sciences, occurs repeatedly. He points out that both quantum mechanics and astronomy work with models. "These models," says Van Peursen, "are not 'pictures' of reality; they only intend to make it understandable."[5]

Apart from whether speaking about a model indicates a direct relation between Van Peursen and Kuitert, it seems that what Van Peursen understands by a model is precisely what Kuitert means by this term. When he calls Adam a "teaching model," he intends to make clear that in all the New Testament says about Adam we do not have a "picture" of the reality of Adam but (only) an illustration, an explanation of the reality of Jesus as Messiah.

Thus speaking of a teaching model contains two inter-related elements. First, the teaching model always serves to illustrate, so that it always points away from itself. The second element is that the teaching model has no independent significance apart from what it intends to illustrate, so the historical aspect is entirely missing from it, or at least can be missing.

It has to be said that the concept "teaching model" is not a felicitous choice, if it is used with reference to the New Testament. The concept calls up clear associations with the concept "model" as employed in the natural sciences, and perhaps has been borrowed directly from them. The concept is scarcely compatible with the language of the New Testament and cannot be considered useful for letting the New Testament say what it intends to say.

5. C. A. Van Peursen, *Filosofische orientatie* (Kampen, 1958), 155.

Many have the same view as Kuitert of the way the New Testament speaks of Adam, although they do not use the concept "teaching model" with reference to Adam. Two recent studies from Roman Catholic circles may be used as examples.

In *The New Catechism*, which is a "declaration of the faith for adults" and was published by order of the bishops in the Netherlands, how Adam is to be spoken of comes up for discussion. *The New Catechism* starts from an evolutionary picture of the world. In the development of our earthly reality, different phases are to be recognized; concerning these, "Nearly everything is uncertain: dates and points in time, the interrelationships between phases. Only an unexpected line stands out with ever greater certainty: a species of animal, living in trees and plains, ascends in a slow development (evolution) to . . . us."[6] Thus Genesis 1–3 does not give us a description of the beginning of things. Nor does the New Testament make an exception on this point, not even what Paul says in Romans 5. "At first sight" it may have the appearance that in Romans 5 Paul intends to emphasize the fact that through one man sin has come into the world. "But this echo of the word 'one,' corresponding to the world view of that time in which Paul took his point of departure, is a literary form, not his message."[7] Thus *The New Catechism* too will not admit to an Adam who, as a historical person, stands at the beginning of the history of humanity. Adam serves only to illustrate the message concerning Jesus.[8]

6. *De nieuwe katechismus* (Hilversum, 1966), 13.

7. Ibid., 308.

8. With reference to Rom. 5:12–21, then, *The New Catechism*, 308, concludes: "The message in this difficult passage is this: how much sin, along with death, reigns in humanity, and how much grace, restoration, along with eternal life, has come in greater abundance through Jesus."

We find the same ideas expressed in the strongest terms in a study, *Adam und Christus*, by the German Roman Catholic theologian P. Lengsfeld. When in Romans 5:14 Paul calls Adam a type of Christ, according to Lengsfeld he makes use of this typological conception to achieve a certain end. That means the typology is not an end in itself but a means and tool. The only point of the typology is to explicate the Christ event for Christians.[9] Therefore, nothing can be read into the typology concerning the historical individuality of the figure of Adam. Paul neither intended nor was able to make historical pronouncements about Adam and his descendants. He intended with the help of Adam simply to explicate the Christ event, that is, he was only interested in the "role" of Adam as the porter who opened the door for the entrance of the dominion of sin, in order to be able to accentuate more sharply the function of Adam as the type of Christ, who establishes the dominion of grace. For Paul the point in the figure of Adam is the "typical" factor and not the historical reality of a man from whom all other men are descended biologically.[10] Thus for Lengsfeld, Adam as a historical person and Adam in his explicating significance with reference to the Christ event come to stand in competition.

To answer the question whether Adam is spoken of in the New Testament as a teaching model in the sense understood by Kuitert—for the purpose of clarifying the message concerning Christ so that the historical element is of no significance—we

9. P. Lengsfeld, *Adam und Christus. Die Adam-Christus-Typologie im Neuen Testament und ihre dogmatische Verwendung bei M. J. Scheeben und K. Barth* (Essen, 1965), 218–21.

10. Ibid., 115ff.

want now to turn to the New Testament itself. In doing so we will confine ourselves to the texts and passages where Adam is mentioned explicitly.[11] We begin with Romans 5:12–21 because, as we have seen, this passage occupies the central place in the discussion concerning Adam as a teaching model.

---

11. Texts in which Adam is not mentioned by name but which also could be discussed in this connection are, e.g., Matt. 19:4 and Acts 17:26.

2

THE DATA OF ROMANS 5:12–21

ADAM AS A TYPE OF CHRIST

In Romans 5:14, Paul gives a description of the relation in which Adam stands to Christ. There he calls Adam the "pattern" or "image" of Christ.[1]

The word in the original Greek is *tupos*, from which our word "type" derives. The word *tupos* comes from a verb that means "strike." *Tupos*, however, did not take on the meaning "blow," but rather the meaning of what is left by a blow, that is, "impression," "imprint," "statuette" (small work of sculpture). The word also takes on the meaning of the "mold" with which an impression, imprint, or statuette is made. Thus it can have the derivative sense of "pattern."[2]

---

1. When Paul speaks about "the image of the one to come," undoubtedly "the one to come" means Christ. See, e.g., A. Nygren, *Commentary on Romans* (Philadelphia, 1949), 217; O. Michel, *Der Brief an die Römer* (Göttingen, 1963), 140; J. Murray, *The Epistle to the Romans*, I (London-Edinburgh, 1967), 188. Cf., however, J. A. T. Robinson, *The Body. A Study in Pauline Theology* (London, 1963), 35n1, according to whom the words "the one to come" do not have reference to Christ but to Moses, or more generally to "the man under the law," or perhaps even simply to "the future."

2. Cf. L. Goppelt, *TDNT*, 8:246–47. Cf. also W. P. DeBoer, *The Imitation of Paul. An Exegetical Study* (Kampen, 1962), 1–23.

The word *tupos* is found in the New Testament in these different senses. It is used to refer to the marks left in Jesus' hands by the nails used at the crucifixion (John 20:25); to images of false gods (Acts 7:43); to the all-determining norm of the instruction that Paul gave (Rom. 6:17); to the pattern the church must follow and by which it is to be determined (Phil. 3:17; 1 Thess. 1:7; 2 Thess. 3:9; 1 Peter 5:3). When *tupos* is used in Romans 5:14 it has kept something of its original meaning. That Adam is called a *tupos* of Christ means that Adam and Christ are related as the mold in which a statuette is cast and the statuette itself.[3] As a *tupos* of Christ, Adam is the "prefiguration" of Christ.

It is already clear that calling Adam a type of Christ expresses more than an accidental correspondence between Adam and Christ. The relationship of type (Adam) and antitype (Christ) involves a fixed correspondence, in the same way that the correspondence between a mold in which a statuette is cast and the statuette itself is not arbitrary but fixed. The mold is oriented to the statuette and finds realization in it. The correspondence between type and antitype in Romans 5:14 is accordingly the correspondence between promise and fulfillment, between "old" and "new" (if we take the words "old" and "new" in the sense they occur particularly in the letter to the Hebrews[4]). This is at the same time an indication that to speak about a "type" is to speak in redemptive-historical categories. Herman Ridderbos says correctly that Adam as type points to Christ "in a previously established redemptive-historical correlation."[5] This

3. L. Goppelt, *Typos. The Typological Interpretation of the Old Testament in the New* (Grand Rapids, 1982), 129; cf. Goppelt, *TDNT*, 8:252.

4. Cf. J. de Vuyst, "Oud en nieuw verbond" in *de brief aan de Hebreeen* (Kampen, 1964), 254ff.

5. H. N. Ridderbos, *Aan de Romeinen* (Kampen, 1959), 116.

redemptive-historical correlation gives speaking about a "type" its true character. As Goppelt says, "Adam is not only an illustrative figure. [Paul] views Adam through Christ as a type in redemptive history, as a prophetic personality placed in Scripture by God. This is the only way he can draw certain conclusions from the relationship of Adam to Christ as conclusions that are founded on a typology."[6] Thus a type always stands at a particular moment in the history of redemption and points away to another (later) moment in the same history. To make use once again of the words of Goppelt, we can say that it is appropriate to speak of a type when particular persons, actions, or events are considered to be "divinely ordained representations or types of future realities that will be even greater and more complete."[7]

So there is a clear difference between biblical typology and allegory. The object of allegorical exegesis is not the facts or the literal sense of a narrative. Alongside the evident meaning of the text or occasionally even in disregard of that meaning, allegorical exegesis seeks to give a "deeper sense." In contrast, typology lets history be history. Consequently, E. E. Ellis correctly points out three factors as determinative for New Testament typology.

The first factor is that a type is not to be thought of apart from God's saving activity in (redemptive) *history*. According to Ellis, the typological exegesis of the New Testament is firmly anchored in the significance that types have in history.[8] Goppelt especially emphasizes this factor. He says that Old Testament types involve a self-revelation of God for which he made use of historical events.

6. Goppelt, *Typos*, 130.
7. Ibid., 18.
8. E. E. Ellis, *Paul's Use of the Old Testament* (Edinburgh-London, 1957), 127.

This self-revelation of God is borne by the Word of God and known in faith. According to its essence, Goppelt says, it is not to be detached from historical events and only holds true in this framework and not as timeless truth. Therefore it can also have a significance for other situations only with due regard for these historical events.[9]

The second factor that Ellis points to as determinative for New Testament typology is that the connection between type and antitype is determined by *God's plan of redemption*.[10] This second factor has to be mentioned directly in unbreakable connection with the first. The significance of a type certainly does not lie in history itself, as if the connection between type and antitype is given with the unchanging regularity of history. G. N. Lammens is correct in saying that the connection between type and antitype is due "to the *constant* at work in history of the *faithfulness of Jahweh*, who remembers his covenant and who continues his work of salvation again and again in new deeds that surpass earlier ones."[11]

To speak typologically, therefore, has nothing to do with cyclical thinking whereby one takes the position that the same thing recurs again and again. The end, then, enables one to see the reproduction of the beginning. Cyclical thinking does not talk about the progress or consummation of history. There is only the circular course of the recurrence and repetition of what already was. Rudolf Bultmann, for example, wants to give refer-

9. L. Goppelt, "Apokalyptik und Typologie bei Paulus," *Christologie und Ethik. Aufsätze zum Neuen Testament* (Göttingen, 1968), 261. See also L. Floor, *De nieuwe exodus: Representatie en inkorporatie in het Nieuwe Testament* (Potchefstroom, 1969), 13.

10. Ellis, *Paul's Use of the Old Testament*, 127–28.

11. G. N. Lammens, *Tot Zijn gedachtenis* (Kampen, 1968), 147.

ences to Adam as a type their place in the framework of cyclical thinking. It is striking that to do this he appeals primarily to one of the Apostolic Fathers.[12] As a matter of fact we do find traces of cyclical thinking in the Apostolic Fathers, whereby types only form historical analogies. Goppelt has shown, however, that with respect to the typology of the New Testament, typology in the Apostolic Fathers is essentially different in character.[13] In the New Testament, the connection between type and antitype is more than a matter of historical analogy. The plus factor lies in the redemptive plan of God, which connects type and antitype.[14]

When, for example, in 1 Corinthians 10:11, Paul says the events associated with the exodus from Egypt have "typical" significance for new covenant believers, "on whom the end of the ages has come," he intends to indicate that God's dealing with his people under the new dispensation corresponds to God's dealing with his people under the old dispensation. The same faithfulness of God comes to expression, both toward the people of the old dispensation and toward the people of the new dispensation. It is not (only) a matter of external similarities between events but (above all) a matter of the essential sameness of God's activity. So the passage of Israel through the Red Sea is not only a type of baptism, because both involve passing through water, but above all because both speak of God's saving activity on which alone a

---

12. Barnabas 6:13; cf. R. Bultmann, "Ursprung und Sinn der Typologie als hermeneutischer Methode," *Exegetica. Aufsätze zur Erforschung des Neuen Testaments* (ed. E. Dinkler, Tübingen, 1967), 370.

13. Goppelt, *TDNT*, 8:256.

14. Cf. Goppelt, *Christologie und Ethik*, 249: "The term designates a connection that is established by God's plan of salvation: *God's plan gives his saving activity* in the area of promise *the same characteristics* it has in fulfillment (Rom. 9:6; 11:29; cf. Eph. 3)."

place among his people can be based.[15] Because the new dispensation involves a saving activity of God in which "the end of the ages" become visible, unbelief and disobedience are all the worse. Types always involve historical events that nevertheless—because the faithfulness of God perseveres —bear in themselves a significance that points beyond the historical fact that once happened to another occurrence.[16]

The third factor determinative for New Testament typology, according to Ellis, is that the Old Testament type and its corresponding New Testament fact belong to two different *dispensations*. The relation of type and antitype is only to be understood within the framework of the divine economy of salvation, the divine dispensation of salvation. "New Testament typology therefore gives," so Ellis says, "not only striking resemblances or analogies but points to a relationship given in the Divine economy of redemption." That holds, according to Ellis, not only for the typology of the exodus from Egypt, in which the two dispensations are expressly contrasted, but equally for the other Old Testament types.[17] The fact that type and antitype are connected with different dispensations of salvation involves the redemptive-historical progression from type to antitype. To speak about a type is to speak about the fulfillment of the old dispensation through the new.[18]

15. Cf. Goppelt, *TDNT*, 8:251–52. See also Ellis, *Paul's Use of the Old Testament*, 127, and Floor, *De nieuwe exodus*, 129.

16. See Goppelt, *Christologie und Ethik*, 262. See also J. Moltmann, "Exegese und Eschatologie der Geschichte," *Evangelische Theologie* 22 (1962): 61.

17. Ellis, *Paul's Use of the Old Testament*, 128. Cf. also L. Floor, *De nieuwe exodus*, 13: "For the typological explanation of the New Testament . . . the organic connection with the Old Testament is . . . of decisive importance."

18. O. Cullmann, *Salvation in History* (New York and Evanston, 1967), 133.

At the same time, to speak typologically indicates that fulfillment does not take place along a straight line. Every straight line is broken through by a repeated falling away that comes from the sin of man. That does not alter the fact that there is a line and that there is progress and fulfillment. Perhaps in this connection we can speak with Cullmann of a "fluctuating line."[19] Lammens also rightly says, "Between the Old Testament history of salvation and its fulfillment in the messianic reality run all sorts of underground lines of connection. . . . We could say that the history of salvation comes to pass *in a progressive spiral movement*."[20] Thus, fundamental to typological language is the fact that it indicates the relation of two moments from the *history* of redemption.

Kuitert attempts to weaken the historical character of the references to Adam as a type by referring to 1 Corinthians 10:4, where within a typological framework we read about a rock that went along with the people of Israel through the wilderness and was Christ. Then Kuitert says:

> What a remarkable observation—made in passing—Paul makes here. For a long time interpreters did not know what to make of it. For we do not read anything in the Old Testament about a rock that travelled along with the people of Israel to provide water. We do read of "water from the rock," and of a rock that Moses struck (Ex. 17:6), but we read nothing of a rock that travelled along with Israel. No, but we do read about it in the big storybooks of the Rabbis! These books tell us about a rock that went along with Israel through the wilderness, and

19. Ibid., 15.
20. Lammens, *Tot Zijn gedachtenis*.

use the story to explain how the water-out-of-the-rock episode could be repeated (compare Exodus 17; Numbers 20:7–13; and Numbers 21:16–18). Paul evidently took this story over from the Rabbis. After all, he knew the rabbinic tradition from his childhood.[21]

"Was this really history for Paul?" Kuitert wonders. He does not hesitate long about the answer. For Kuitert it is clear that the question concerning what is historical or what is nonhistorical was not a question for Paul here, because he used the story in the service of his teaching about Jesus.

The argument of Kuitert seems fairly strong: If in 1 Corinthians 10:1–11 a verse is present in which historical realities are treated in such a surprising way, while this section still clearly intends to be typology and the word "type" is even expressly mentioned, can and may the historical element in a type be given so strong an accent as frequently happens and as we also have done in the preceding discussion?

Still, this argument appears to be more than it is. It should be pointed out that Paul's explanation for the rock accompanying Israel is that that rock was Christ. Therefore we will have to think in another direction than Kuitert does. Goppelt points out that the conception of Paul in 1 Corinthians 10:4 comes especially close to the conception that we find in a Jewish explanation of Exodus 17:6. That explanation says that wherever Israel turns, God will come along in order to supply water for his people, whereby "in some respect" God is thus called the rock accompanying

21. Kuitert, op. cit. Cf. also M. Boertien, "De joodse achtergrond van het parallel Adam/Christus in het N.T.," *Gereformeerde Theologisch Tijdschrift* 68 (1968): 217.

his people.[22] According to Goppelt, who refers to 1 Corinthians 8:6, Paul now intends to point to Christ as the mediator in the redemptive event mentioned in 1 Corinthians 10:4.[23] The rock that followed the people of Israel was, as Paul expressly says, a "spiritual" rock, namely, Christ. If Paul is taking over a rabbinic midrash, he transposes it in such a way that it takes on for him a significance entirely his own. Paul means to say that the benefits that were received in the old dispensation were already benefits of Christ, and he warns the Corinthians not to despise those benefits in unbelief and disobedience as the fathers did.[24] We may conclude that Paul is definitely recalling historical facts, and in that account uses a metaphor, a figure of speech. But that figure, a word play, does not alter the fact that the apostle writes about historical facts. Not for a moment was he thinking about a literal wandering rock in the Sinai desert.

The One

Again and again in Romans 5:12–21 we encounter the word "one." This word recurs as an echo in nearly every verse. The typological correspondence between Adam and Christ is concentrated in this word. The relevant statements are the following:

22. Goppelt, *Typos*, 146. Cf. also H. L. Strack and P. Billerbeck, *Kommentar zum Neuen Testament aus Talmud und Midrasch* (München, 1926), 3:408. The reference is to Mekelta Ex. 17:6. See further F. J. Pop, *De eerste brief van Paulus aan de Corinthiërs* (Nijkerk, 1965), 198, according to whom the point of the Jewish tradition concerning the accompanying rock is nothing other than to give expression "to Jahweh's accompanying his people and his continual care for them."

23. Goppelt, *Typos*, 146.

24. Cf. F. W. Grosheide, *Commentary on the First Epistle to the Corinthians* (Grand Rapids, 1953), 221–22; Pop, *De eerste brief van Paulus aan de Corinthiërs*, 198–99.

STATEMENTS ABOUT ADAM:	STATEMENTS ABOUT CHRIST:
"As sin came into the world *through one man*" (verse 12)	
"For if many died *by one man's trespass*" (verse 15)	"Much more have the grace of God and the free gift *by the grace of that one man*, Jesus Christ, abounded for many" (verse 15)
"And the free gift is not like the result of that *one man's sin*." (verse 16)	
"For the judgment following *one trespass* brought condemnation" (verse 16)	
"If, *because of one man's trespass*, death reigned *through that one man*" (verse 17)	"Much more shall those . . . reign in life *through the one man*, Jesus Christ" (verse 17)
"As *one trespass* led to condemnation for all men" (verse 18)	"So *one act of righteousness* leads to justification and life for all men." (verse 18)
"As *by the one man's disobedience* the many were made sinners" (verse 19)	"So *by the one man's obedience* the many will be made righteous." (verse 19)

From these parallel statements about Adam and Christ, it is clear that Adam as "the one" and Christ as "the one" are not placed next to each other on the same line as equals. Christ as "the one" towers far above Adam as "the one." The emphasis here has been correctly placed, for example, by G. C. Berkouwer, who says Paul "did not make a simple analogy between Adam and Christ, as though Christ merely restores what was once broken in Adam." In this connection he refers to Romans 5:15 where Paul says the gift of grace is *not* like the transgression.[25] Paul wishes to point out the superabundance of grace. Romans 5:12–21 is a *doxology* in which the theme already sounded in the first eleven verses of the chapter is further elaborated. "Within that context of the 'superfluidity of grace' Paul now speaks of Adam."[26]

Within the framework of this disparity between Adam and Christ, however, a decisive correspondence between the two must be recognized. That correspondence lies in the position that each occupies as "the one."[27] Both Adam and Christ occupy a unique position with respect to all who belong to them. Their actions, the act of disobedience and the act of obedience (verse 18), respectively, are decisive for all who belong to them. Ridderbos rightly observes that just as "the one" through whom sin and death have entered the world, Adam is a type of the one to come.[28] To use the words of W. H. Velema, in the case of both Adam and Christ it is a matter of a particular structure, namely, the structure of the "all through one." "Paul thus sees the same law between Christ and his people as he has observed between Adam and humanity."[29] In the words of the South African, I. J. du Plessis, Adam is "not simply a symbolic allegory. Just as the head of humanity he forms the counterpart to Christ."[30]

25. G. C. Berkouwer, *Sin* (Grand Rapids, 1971), 508 (modified in light of the Dutch original). See also Nygren, *Commentary on Romans*, 208: not an "Adam redivivus." So also I. J. du Plessis, *Christus as Hoof van Kerk en Kosmos* (Groningen, 1962), 36; O. Michel, *Der Brief an die Römer*, 140–41.

26. Berkouwer, *Sin*, 509. Cf. also W. H. Velema, *Verkenningen in Romeinen* (Den Haag, 1962), 40.

27. De Vuyst ("Oud en nieuw verbond," 197n242) correctly observes that Paul draws a parallel between Adam and Christ in view of their different positions as "one" for "all," but not in view of the different grounds on which these respective positions rest.

28. H. N. Ridderbos, *Paul*, trans. J. R. de Witt (Grand Rapids, 1975), 96, 98.

29. Velema, *Verkenningen in Romeinen*, 40.

30. Du Plessis, *Christus as Hoof van Kerk en Kosmos*, 36.

This correspondence between Adam and Christ in their position as "the one" in contrast with all who belong to them is flatly denied by Karl Barth in a study devoted to Romans 5:12–21. According to Barth, in this passage Paul's intention is to speak about the human nature of Christ in order to make clear what is the secret and the truth of human nature as such. For Paul, the reality of Christ comes up for discussion as a "space" or "territory" in which man as such finds himself, thus even the man who wishes to know nothing of Christ. Human nature as such is encompassed by the humanity of Christ. Thus we have to seek the key to the secret of man as such in the humanity of Christ.[31] In this light then Barth defines the relationship of Adam and Christ to each other. Adam, who is apparently the first, is in reality the second, and Christ, who is apparently the second, is in reality the first. In terminology taken from 1 Corinthians 15:47, it can also be said that Christ as the first is "above" and Adam as the second is "below." Because Christ is "above," humanity is contained in him as a unity and humanity belongs to him. Christ is then also the head of humanity, while Adam is head in appearance only. As the one who is "below," Adam cannot be head. Only he who is "above" can be that.[32] In reality Adam is "primus inter pares," one among many. What Adam was, we are too as are all who after Adam and with us are called "men." The converse also holds: what we and all men are, the one Adam also already was and is. Man is both a distinct individual and also, as such, together with all others, representative of all. Man is always for himself

31. K. Barth, *Christus und Adam, nach Rom. 5. Ein Beitrag zur Frage nach dem Menschen und der Menschheit* (Zürich, 1952), 50ff.
32. Ibid., 15, 31.

and always for all. Thus as a matter of fact Adam can represent all other men, but he can do that only in the same way in which all others also can represent him. Thus Adam cannot determine the history of other men. He only does as first what all do after him.[33] Adam and all other men are on the same level, namely, "below." A position of Adam in contrast with all other men is out of the question.

It has been pointed out correctly that in his study of Romans 5:12–21, Barth's point of departure is wrong. He wishes to find in this passage a pronouncement about humanity as such. The light, however, does not fall on the being of Adam, as if he thereby represents and reveals the being of all other men. Nor is the point the human nature of Christ as the key to the secret of human nature as such.[34] All emphasis falls on two different acts, namely, the act of disobedience on the one hand and the act of obedience on the other, whereby all reflection about an ontological priority is entirely outside Paul's purview. P. Lengsfeld is right when he says that Barth has just as little room for responsible acts at the beginning of history as he has for Christ's act of obedience. The antithesis between obedience and disobedience becomes nothing else than a reflex of ontic orders of different worth. Present in Barth is a depreciation of the historical dimension in favor of the conception of two different spheres, namely, what is "above" and what is "below."[35]

It seems that Barth says the opposite of what Paul says. For Barth, Adam is only "primus inter pares," one among many. For Paul, Adam

---

33. Ibid., 53ff.

34. Cf. E. Brandenburger, *Adam und Christus. Exegetisch-religionsgeschichtliche Untersuchung zu Römer 5:12–21 (I. Kor. 15)* (Neukirchen, 1962), 270.

35. Lengsfeld, *Adam und Christus*, 188.

is "the one" who acts in a way that is unrepeatable for all who belong to him, and whose act is determinative for all who belong to him. Barth is correct in pointing out that there is a disparity between Adam and Christ. Earlier we too came to the conclusion that Adam as "the one" and Christ as "the one" are not placed next to each other on the same line as equals. The question, however, is in what this disparity consists. For Paul it clearly lies in the difference between the act of Adam and that of Christ. The disparity between Adam and Christ is that between the act of disobedience and the act of obedience with their outcomes, death as the consequence of disobedience and life as the consequence of obedience. For Barth this disparity is of a different character. For him it is connected with a disparity in order or a disparity of two spheres, namely, what is "above" and what is "below." With E. Brandenburger we should say that for Paul the point is two mutually exclusive antitheses and, in fact, in an irreversible historical sequence, while for Barth the point is orders of different worth. Brandenburger then can also—rightly —come to no other conclusion than that in Romans 5 Paul speaks of Adam as the first historical man, who thus also stands in a historical relation to his descendants.[36]

Worth mentioning further is the sharp criticism that Bultmann has leveled at the view of Barth. If for Barth Adam is not the head of humanity but "one among many" who as such represents humanity, according to Bultmann, Adam has become to all intents and purposes the idea of man.[37] This cannot be maintained without consequences. Just as the figure of Adam becomes the idea of "man," so Christ too, according to Bultmann, appears to become

36. Brandenburger, *Adam und Christus*, 272–73.
37. R. Bultmann, "Adam und Christus nach Römer 5," *Exegetica. Aufsätze zur Erforschung des Neuen Testaments*, ed. E. Dinkler (Tübingen, 1967), 444. Bultmann calls that demythologization "in a questionable way."

an idea. When Christ is called the "true man" by Barth, he is still not the concrete historical man but the idea of the "true" man. To us this criticism of Bultmann seems to the point, although we will just as little be able to follow his own view of Romans 5:12–21.[38]

The same error that Barth makes is also made by Kuitert. He also maintains that in Romans 5:12–21 Paul speaks of Adam as the *first* transgressor. He says, "In Romans 5:12ff., it is essential to Paul's argument that Adam was the first sinner. . . . Paul's whole argument hinges on Adam as the first sinner."[39] As the first transgressor, Adam is clearly placed beside all other men as transgressors. In Adam as the first becomes visible what lives in all men. Thus Kuitert too misunderstands the real point of Romans 5:12–21. For we saw that for Paul in this passage the disobedience of Adam is not merely illustrative for all other men but is determinative for all other men. It has been correctly pointed out that the word "first" (sinner) does not occur in the whole of Romans 5. Here Adam is characterized as "the one" who occupies a unique position, by which his act of disobedience is of decisive significance for all who belong to him. "Whether someone is the first to sin or sins as the head of a community and so opens the door for the consequence of sin, death, upon his descendants are two different matters."[40]

If it be asked in what sense the act of Adam and that of Christ can be of decisive significance for all who belong to them, we can

38. Cf. ibid., 434, where he maintains that in Romans 5:12 Paul is reaching toward the gnostic myth of the primal man. See also Bultmann, *Theology of the New Testament* (New York, 1951), 1:251. For a rebuttal of this idea of Bultmann see Ridderbos, *Paul*, 32–35.

39. Ridderbos, *Paul*, 40.

40. C. Gilhuis, "Kritische kanttekeningen op Kuitert," *Gereformeerd Weekblad* 24 (1969): 182. Cf. also J. Helderman, "Ingezonden," *Gereformeerd Weekblad* 24 (1969): 199. See further du Plessis, *Christus as Hoof van Kerk en Kosmos*, 36.

refer to the idea of representation. Adam and Christ can both be called "the one," because both as heads of a humanity that belongs to them—the old humanity and the new humanity, respectively—represent in a unique way the humanity belonging to them.

Verses 13 and 14 especially point in the direction of representation. Paul asserts in these verses that in the period from Adam to Moses, when as yet there was no law, there could be no question of transgressing in the same way as Adam. We will certainly have to understand by this that in the period from Adam to Moses men were not under a clear commandment with a clear threat of punishment, as was the case with Adam and was once more the case when the law was given to Moses.[41]

Incidentally, with the words "from Adam to Moses" Paul is obviously thinking of a fixed portion of time, a given historical period. Adam stands at the beginning of that period, Moses at the end. As surely as a historical terminus is in view in the case of Moses, a historical starting point is in view in the case of Adam. It is inconceivable that for a fixed portion of time that is clearly intended as a historical period, Paul would have in mind a historical terminus (Moses) and not a historical starting point.[42]

In the period from Adam to Moses, when there was no law and so also no transgression in the same way as Adam, death still reigned as king. To this Paul prefaces the words that, even before the law, sin was already present but that sin is not imputed when there is no law. No other conclusion is possible than this: by sin

41. Cf. Ridderbos, *Romeinen*, 116; A. F. N. Lekkerkerker, *De brief van Paulus aan de Romeinen* (Nijkerk, 1962), 1:244.
42. So, e.g., John Murray, *The Epistle to the Romans*, I (London-Edinburgh, 1967), 1:190, speaks about a "segment of history." A different view is taken by F. J. Leenhardt, *L'Épître de Saint Paul aux Romains* (Neuchâtel-Paris, 1957), 85n2.

before the law Paul does not mean the actual sins committed by men but the sin of Adam as "the one" in the decisive significance that sin has for all who belong to him. It is to that sin that death is due as the punishment on sin in the period from Adam to Moses. Ridderbos rightly says that in verses 13 and 14 Adam has the significance of "representative-for-all" and that in this significance he is a type of the one to come.[43]

The closing words of verse 12 also become clear from verses 13 and 14. The last part of verse 12 says: ". . . and so death came to all men, because all sinned." These words do not have reference to the personal, actual sins of all but to all being reckoned as sinners on the basis of the sin of Adam. If we would be forced to think of personal, actual sins in the conclusion of verse 12, it would be in contradiction with what is said earlier in verse 12. Moreover, there is then a contradiction with verses 13 and 14. Bultmann, who chooses to understand the conclusion of verse 12 in the sense of personal, actual sins, therefore calls verse 13 "completely incomprehensible,"[44] and elsewhere he speaks of "confusion" in the text.[45] On the basis of what precedes and what follows, in the conclusion of verse 12 we shall have to think of death as the punishment and imputation of the sin of Adam. Because in his sinning Adam was the representative of all men, his sin is of decisive significance for all men.[46]

Verse 19 also points further in the direction of representation. Here the verbs usually translated "were made" and "will be

---

43. Ridderbos, *Romeinen*, 116. Cf. also Ridderbos, *Paul*, 96ff. See further Nygren, *Commentary on Romans*, 214–15; Murray, *Romans*, 190–91.

44. Bultmann, *Theology*, 1:252.

45. Bultmann, *Exegetica*, 433.

46. Cf. Ridderbos, *Romeinen*, 115ff.; Murray, *Romans*, 184ff.

made" can also be rendered by "were constituted" and "will be constituted." In the context taken as a whole, this last rendering seems more accurate. The verb used here will have to be understood in the same sense in which it is to be understood in the Septuagint[47] of Deuteronomy 25:6. There the verb occurs with reference to the son born from a levirate marriage who must carry on the name of the deceased husband. The son counts and is reckoned as the son of the first husband, not on the ground of what he is but on the ground of his status before the law.[48] So also in Romans 5:19 it is a matter of "being constituted" sinners and righteous respectively, in the sense of being reckoned as such according to the judgment of God. When the context as a whole is surveyed, the thought cannot be the personal sin of the "sinners" or the personal (moral) righteousness of the "righteous."[49] In the entire section preceding verse 19, "justification" and "righteousness" are spoken of only in the sense of a gift imputed by God. Likewise, being constituted "sinners" in the sense of being reckoned as sinners connects with what is said in the preceding verses about the decisive significance of the sin of Adam for all who belong to him.[50] If we ask ourselves how we are to conceive of this "being constituted," we can say with Ridderbos: "Again everything comes down to the fact of

47. The Septuagint is an ancient Greek translation of the Old Testament.

48. Cf. Ridderbos, *Romeinen*, 122.

49. So, for example, Berkouwer, *Sin*, 499ff. A. Oepke (*TDNT*, 3:445–46) provides a combination of the forensic and ethical views when he speaks about "virtual" sin and righteousness (in Adam and Christ) and about an "actual" existence as sinner and righteous in the ethical sense of the word.

50. Cf. S. Greijdanus, *De brief van den apostel Paulus aan de gemeente te Rome* (Amsterdam, 1933), 1:289–90; J. A. C. Van Leeuwen–D. Jacobs, *De brief aan de Romeinen* (Kampen, 1952), 118–19; Ellis, *Paul's Use of the Old Testament*, 60; Ridderbos, *Romeinen*, 122; idem., *Paul*, 98ff.

the many being represented in the one man Adam and the one man Christ."[51]

In our opinion the representation of "the many" through "the one" is not to be grounded in the "corporate solidarity" of "the many" with "the one." The expression "corporate solidarity" is intended to indicate that "the many" are incorporated and included in "the one." "The one" therefore can be described as a "corporate personality." It was above all H. W. Robinson who has caused this conception to find general acceptance in exegesis. Robinson considers it also of the greatest significance for understanding what Paul says about Adam and Christ in Romans 5:12–21.[52] Invariably present in this conception of "corporate personality," however, is a kind of reciprocity between "the one" (the corporate personality) and "the many" (all who are incorporated and included in him). "The one" and "the many," as Robinson says, flow over into each other. What is said of "the one" can be said of "the many," and so can *the reverse*.[53] This "reciprocity" between "the one" and "the many" and this "vice versa" of "the one" and "the many," however, are not present in the idea of representation in Romans 5:12–21. There "the one" determines "the many," while there is no question of a reverse determination.[54] In addition, the concept "corporate" expresses an existing reality. If someone is incorporated and included in a corporate personality, then he is considered to be actually present in a certain way

51. Ridderbos, *Romeinen*, 122.

52. H. W. Robinson, "The Hebrew Conception of Corporate Personality," *Werden und Wesen des Alten Testament* [*Zeitschrift für die altestamentliche Wissenschaft*, 66 (1936)]:57.

53. Robinson, "The Hebrew Conception of Corporate Personality," 53: There is a "fluidity of transition from the individual to the society and vice versa."

54. Cf. also Floor, *De nieuwe exodus*, 165–66.

in the corporate personality.[55] It is clear then that the concept "corporate" is hardly to be associated with the concept of representation, especially if representation is conceived of, as we did, in the sense of "being reckoned." G. C. Berkouwer rightly says, "With this being *reckoned* as a *forensic* judgment the corporate (as a reality) is precluded and in principle abrogated, at least if one relates imputation to what was not real."[56] With L. Floor we can assert "that the use of the word 'corporate' ought to be avoided when it is a question of the idea of representation."[57]

The representation of "the many" through "the one" does not rest in the corporate solidarity of "the many" with "the one," but in a structure ordained by God. Herman Ridderbos has correctly pointed in this direction when he says that the unity of Adam and his descendants rests "upon a God-ordained structure in the creation and redemption of the human race."[58] That Adam's act of disobedience as "the one" holds for all who belong to him finds its cause in the fact that God has so determined that what "the one" has done is imputed to "the many." The same thing is to be said regarding Christ's act of obedience as "the one" with reference to all who belong to him.

In this respect what we already saw as characteristic of Adam as a type of Christ comes to its full right. In Christ, God maintains in sovereign faithfulness the structure of "all through one" which he put into effect with Adam. In Christ God also causes

55. For a forceful example of this, cf. Robinson ("The Hebrew Conception of Corporate Personality," 49ff., 54, 58ff.). Robinson speaks repeatedly in this connection of a physical presence of "the many" in "the one." Cf. esp. 52.

56. Berkouwer, *Sin*, 517 (modified in light of the Dutch original).

57. Floor, *De nieuwe exodus*, 166.

58. Ridderbos, *Romeinen*, 114.

this structure to reach its richest fulfillment. Just in this way Adam is a type of Christ.

It ought to be clear that the characterization of Adam as a "teaching model" in no way does justice to the representation idea that assumes such a central place in Romans 5:12–21. If someone functions as a teaching model, there can be no speaking of the unique position of such a person. The position of Adam is unique, namely the position of "the one," the representative head of the old humanity. Thereby the idea of a teaching model—at least what concerns Romans 5:12–21—is entirely excluded.

We may now consider more briefly other New Testament texts that speak of Adam.

3

OTHER NEW TESTAMENT DATA

LUKE 3:38

In Luke 3:38, Adam is mentioned within the framework of the genealogy of Jesus. The last (or if you will, the first) links in the genealogy, mentioned in verse 38, are: "Enos, the son of Seth, the son of Adam, the son of God." Besides the genealogy of Jesus preserved in Luke 3:23–38, a second is handed down to us in Matthew 1:1–16. A comparison of these two genealogies brings to light the difficulty that entirely different names are mentioned for the descendants of David. In Matthew 1 after David, the line continues through his son Solomon (verse 6), and in Luke 3 it continues through his son Nathan (verse 31).

A possible explanation for this difficulty is that Matthew 1 gives us the genealogy of Jesus that follows the ancestors of Joseph, while in Luke 3 the line of the ancestors of Mary is followed.[1]

1. So, e.g., J. de Zwaan, *Het evangelie van Lucas* (Groningen–Den Haag, 1922), 70; N. Geldenhuys, *Commentary on the Gospel of Luke* (London, 1956), 151. So too already in the ancient church, Tatian. An especially interesting explanation is found

Whatever explanation one gives for the different names in the two genealogies, the point that concerns us in this connection is *that* there are definite explanations so that the occurrence of two entirely different genealogies of Jesus in no sense detracts from the historical reliability of both or either one of them. Besides, that would be difficult to square with the fact that at the time the Gospels were written, members of Jesus' family were still living who could have corrected the genealogies.[2] Moreover, it would be difficult to square with the fact that in Jewish circles from the last centuries before Christ and also after Christ, genealogies were attended with the greatest meticulousness. Thus Josephus, a Jewish writer from the first century after Christ, can mention his genealogy as it was officially registered in a public register. Josephus relates also that Jews who were living outside Canaan sent the names of their children to Jerusalem in order to be registered officially.[3]

In their commentary on the New Testament from the Talmud and Midrash, H. L. Strack and P. Billerbeck state that there can be no doubt of the existence of reliable genealogies in the time of the New Testament. Repeatedly in the older Jewish literature these genealogies were explicitly recorded and, in part, also reproduced briefly as to their content.[4]

---

in T. Zahn, *Das Evangelium des Lucas* (Leipzig, 1913), 210–15. Zahn takes the position that both Matthew and Luke present a genealogy of Jesus in the line of Joseph. He refers to a communication of Sextus Julius Africanus (third century), according to whom Joseph's father was both Jacob (mentioned in Matthew 1) and Heli (mentioned in Luke 3) by means of levirate marriage.

2. T. Zahn, *Das Evangelium des Lucas*, 210; Geldenhuys, *Commentary on the Gospel of Luke*, 152.

3. Cf. Geldenhuys, *Commentary on the Gospel of Luke*, 151. Cf. also W. Grundmann, *Das Evangelium nach Lukas* (Berlin, 1961), 111.

4. H. L. Strack and P. Billerbeck, *Kommentar zum Neuen Testament aus Talmud und Midrasch* (München, 1926), 1:4.

In just such a genealogy the name of Adam too is mentioned by Luke. The name of Adam is on a line with all other names. Given the character of the genealogies and the accuracy with which they are attended, it is inconceivable that Luke would have thought about Adam other than as a historical person. That Adam is called the son of God, as Seth, in turn, is called a son of Adam, is to be regarded as an echo of Genesis 5:1–3, where we read that God made Adam in the likeness of God, while Adam begat Seth in his likeness, as his image.

We do not deny that with his rendering of the genealogy of Jesus, Luke has a specific theological purpose and so intends to give more than merely an interesting genealogical fact. That Luke goes back to Adam in the genealogy of Jesus, while Matthew only goes back to Abraham, certainly hangs together with the overall universalistic design of the Gospel that Luke wrote. Luke wanted to make clear Jesus' significance for all kinds of nations and peoples, while Matthew wanted Jesus to be seen above all as the promised Messiah of the Jews. It fits completely into the design of Luke's Gospel that he extends the line back to Adam.[5]

Perhaps, besides this, Luke wished for Jesus to be seen as the second Adam, inaugurator of the new humanity.[6] W. Grundmann

5. Cf. J. Schmid, *Das Evangelium nach Lukas* (Regensburg, 1960), 102; Geldenhuys, *Commentary on the Gospel of Luke*, 153.

6. So Zahn, *Das Evangelium des Lucas*, 220–21; de Zwaan, *Het evangelie van Lucas*, 71; A. Schlatter, *Das Evangelium des Lukas, aus seinen Quellen erklärt* (Stuttgart, 1931), 218–19; A. Schlatter, *Die Evangelien nach Markus und Lukas* (Stuttgart, 1947), 199; Grundmann, *Das Evangelium nach Lukas*, 111. In this connection Zahn also refers to the immediately following section, the temptation in the desert, in which perhaps Jesus is likewise to be thought of as the second Adam, because Jesus stands fast in the temptation in which Adam fell. Cf. Boertien, "De joodse achtergrond van het parallel Adam/Christus in het N.T.," 215. Another view is taken by Schmid, *Das Evangelium nach Lukas*, 102.

thinks that he can also deduce this from the fact that the genealogy in Luke consists of 77 members. He proposes to see in back of this the Jewish scheme of the twelve-week apocalypse. Jesus stands at the end of the eleventh world period and is born as the beginner of the twelfth and last period, the eschatological time. With him the new, eschatological humanity begins.[7]

That the genealogies are not reproduced fully and are stylized in a particular way is clear in Matthew[8] and certainly not impossible in Luke. That a particular scheme underlies Luke's own rendering is thus no more impossible. Whatever theological purpose Luke could have had with his reproduction of the genealogy—and that theological purpose is certainly present—it may never be played off against the authentic character of the genealogy. Characteristic for a genealogy is that it makes reference to historical persons. The theological purpose of Luke does not detract from the authentic character of the genealogy, but is based on that character.

1 Corinthians 15:22, 45

In 1 Corinthians 15, Paul mentions Adam in a context that bears an especially strong resemblance to the context in Romans 5:12–21, where mention is made of Adam. In 1 Corinthians 15:22, Paul says: "For as in Adam all die, so also in Christ shall all be made alive." In verse 45 we read: "Thus it is written: 'The first man Adam became a living being'; the last Adam became a life-giving Spirit." As in Romans 5 so also in 1 Corinthians 15, Adam and Christ are spoken of as representative heads of all who belong to them.

---

7. Grundmann, *Das Evangelium nach Lukas*, 111.
8. Cf., e.g., the omission of specific links in Matt. 1:8.

That is especially clear so far as 1 Corinthians 15:22 is concerned. Adam and Christ are not spoken of as private persons but with an eye to the decisive significance they have for "all." Verse 20 says concerning Christ that he was resurrected from the dead as firstfruits of those who are asleep. The thought of representation is indissolubly connected with the concept "firstfruits."[9] The resurrection of Christ from the dead is of decisive significance for the resurrection of all who are his, because now that Christ has been raised as the representative firstfruits, the future resurrection of all who are his has become not only a possibility but a certainty. In the resurrected Christ as representative firstfruits, the new life of the new creation has already broken through into this dispensation.[10]

In this same framework, reference is also made to Adam. The man through whom death came stands, so far as his position is concerned, on a line with the man through whom the resurrection of the dead came (verse 21). Here Adam too is not characterized as a private person but as the representative head of all who belong to him.[11]

In 1 Corinthians 15:45, Adam and Christ are not spoken of differently than in verse 22. The words in verses 48 and 49 follow on

9. For further argumentation I refer to my address, *Het heden van de toekomst* (Kampen, 1969), 8ff.

10. Thus Ridderbos, *Paul*, 57. Cf. also H. Sasse, *TDNT*, 1:207; N. A. Dahl, *Das Volk Gottes. Eine Untersuchung zum Kirchenbewusstsein des Urchristentums* (Oslo, 1941), 217; N. Q. Hamilton, *The Holy Spirit and Eschatology in Paul* (Edinburgh, 1957), 17; O. Cullmann, *Christ and Time*, rev. ed. (Philadelphia, 1964), 236; H. Schwantes, *Schöpfung der Endzeit. Ein Beitrag zum Verständnis der Auferweckung bei Paulus* (Stuttgart, 1962), 62, 79.

11. Cf. also O. Kuss, *Die Briefe an die Römer, Korinther und Galater* (Regensburg, 1940), 188; J. A. Schep, *The Nature of the Resurrection Body. A Study of the Biblical Data* (Grand Rapids, 1964), 176.

the words in verse 45: "As is the one who is earthly, so are those who are earthly, and as is the one who is heavenly, so are those who are heavenly. And as we have borne the image of the one who is earthly, so shall we bear the image of the one who is heavenly" (author's translation). By the one who is "earthly" is obviously meant the "first man," Adam, and by the one who is "heavenly" the last Adam, Christ (cf. verse 47). Here too Adam and Christ are clearly seen as the representative heads of all who belong to them, namely, those who are "earthly" and those who are "heavenly" respectively.[12] The one who is "earthly," Adam, is determinative for those who are "earthly"; the one who is "heavenly," Christ, is likewise determinative for those who are "heavenly."

We can say the same thing about the references to Adam in 1 Corinthians 15 that we said in connection with Romans 5:12–21. Where Adam is referred to as a representative head, it is not possible to apply to him the qualification "teaching model." That qualification cannot do justice to the unique position of Adam.

It is striking that in verse 45a, where Paul refers to Adam, he expressly calls Adam "the first man, Adam." That is all the more striking because in verse 45a Paul takes over the wording of the Septuagint translation of Genesis 2:7 but adds to it "first" and "Adam." The purpose of these additions is obviously to emphasize that Paul is not referring to "man" in general but to a particular man, namely, to Adam as the man who stood at the beginning of the history of humanity.[13]

12. The expressions "earthly" and "heavenly" are to be taken as designations of quality. With Pop, *De eerste brief van Paulus aan de Corinthiërs*, 397, we will have to take "earthly" in the sense of "perishable," and "heavenly" in the sense of "imperishable," "glorious," "powerful."

13. Thus Schep, *The Nature of the Resurrection Body*, 173. Cf. also Grosheide, *Commentary on the First Epistle to the Corinthians*, 386.

These additions make clear that for Paul, Adam was not merely the model of "man" but a particular man with a particular place in the history of humanity.

One further important matter should be pointed out with reference to 1 Corinthians 15. That is the expression "in Adam," which is used in verse 22 in parallel with the expression "in Christ": "For as in Adam all die, so also in Christ shall all be made alive." The expression "in Christ" or "in Christ Jesus" occurs repeatedly in the letters of Paul[14] and probably underlies the expression "in Adam." The expression "in Adam," then, must be explained by the expression "in Christ."

A. Deissmann was the first to dedicate a detailed study to the expression "in Christ (Jesus)." Deissmann understands the expression in a local sense so that to be "in Christ" means to exist in Christ locally.[15] In this connection Deissmann uses the illustration of the air we inhale such that the air is "in" us and fills us, while at the same time it is "in" that air that we live and breathe.[16] A mystical meaning attaches to this local meaning. Taken just in this local sense, "in Christ" is the typical Pauline expression for the most intimate fellowship imaginable between Christians and the living Christ, according to Deissmann.[17]

The views of Deissmann have had great influence. Although criticism has been directed to the fact that Deissmann "uniformly" explains every place where the expression "in Christ (Jesus)"

14. On Paul's use of this expression, see the study of F. Neugebauer, *In Christo. Eine Untersuchung zum paulinischen Glaubensverstandnis* (Göttingen, 1961).

15. A. Deissmann, *Die neutestamentliche Formel "in Christo Jesu"* (Marburg, 1892), 97.

16. A. Deissmann, *Paulus. Eine kultur- und religionsgeschichtliche Skizze* (Tübingen, 1911), 87.

17. Deissmann, *Formel*, 98.

occurs in a local-mystical sense,[18] in many respects he has been followed on essential points.[19]

In our opinion, the path indicated by Deissmann, so far as both the local and mystical aspects are concerned, is not the path we can follow to explain the expression "in Christ (Jesus)." F. Neugebauer has pointed out a better way. He proposes to take the preposition "in" in the expression "in Christ (Jesus)" neither locally nor mystically but "historically," that is to say, that the preposition has reference to an event.[20] He starts from the fact that Christ (Jesus), to whom the expression "in Christ (Jesus)" refers, is the resurrected Christ, who at the same time is the crucified Christ.[21] On the basis of this starting point Neugebauer can maintain, correctly in our opinion, that "to be" in Christ does not mean an ontological condition but the fact of being determined by the once-for-all work of Christ and having an involvement in that event. This meaning is especially clear in the closing verses of 2 Corinthians 5, above all in the well-known words of verse 17: "Therefore, if anyone is in Christ, he is a new creation." With Neugebauer these words are to be paraphrased: "If anyone is determined by the cross and resurrection of Christ, if he is involved in these events and so died and rose with Christ, then he is a new creation and the old has totally passed away."[22]

18. For criticism on this point, see, e.g., A. Oepke, *TDNT*, 2:541–42; A. Wikenhauser, *Die Christusmystik des Apostels Paulus* (Freiburg, 1956), 7.

19. Thus Wikenhauser (ibid., 9) explicitly subscribes to Deissmann's view of the mystical sense of the expression, while Oepke (*TDNT*, 542) adopts his local conception.

20. Neugebauer, *In Christo*, 148. Cf. also F. Neugebauer, "Das Paulinische 'in Christo,'" *New Testament Studies* 4 (1957–58): 138. The term Neugebauer uses in this connection is "geschichtlich."

21. Neugebauer, *In Christo*, 44ff.

22. Neugebauer, *New Testament Studies* 4, 132. M. Bouttier, *En Christ. étude d'exégèse et de théologie pauliniennes* (Paris, 1962), thinks along the same lines as Neugebauer.

In this sense there is a parallel between the expressions "in Christ" and "in Adam." The expression "in Adam," too, is to be taken neither locally nor mystically. "In Adam" means: "determined by what Adam did."[23] The background here is the idea of Adam as representative head. The qualification "teaching model" cannot do justice to this "historical" significance of the preposition "in." For in a teaching model the historical element does not have decisive significance. As the point at stake in the expression "in Christ (Jesus)" is the fact of being determined by the cross and resurrection of Christ, so the point at stake in the expression "in Adam" is the fact of being determined by the disobedience of Adam, through which death came into the world.

1 Timothy 2:13–14

In 1 Timothy 2 and 3 we find a variety of regulations with respect to congregational life. Not only men but women too are involved in the public worship of the congregation. After Paul has referred to the men in verse 2:8, he continues in verse 9 with the words: "Likewise also . . . women." From this it is apparent that Paul recognizes women "as participants in the gatherings of the congregation no less than men."[24] The woman, however, has her own place in public worship, and that place involves clear limitations. In verses 11 and 12 Paul says: "Let a woman learn quietly with all submissiveness. I do not permit a woman to teach or to exercise authority over a man; rather, she is to remain quiet." The place of the woman implies that she does not give instruction in public worship. For instruction comes to the congregation with

23. See also Schep, *The Nature of the Resurrection Body*, 180, and Ridderbos, *Paul*, 60ff.
24. Thus Ridderbos, *De pastorale brieven* (Kampen, 1967), 85.

authority, and therefore to give instruction would give the woman a position toward the man that is not in keeping with her place as a woman.[25]

Paul goes on following verse 12 to refer to the creation and fall, and uses the names of Adam and Eve. To prove that women may not exercise authority over men by giving instruction in the congregation, Paul brings forward two arguments. We find the first argument in verse 13: "For Adam was formed first, then Eve." The second argument is in verse 14: "And Adam was not deceived, but the woman was deceived and fell into transgression."

This reference to Adam approaches very closely the meaning one intends by using the term "teaching model." The relationship of Adam and Eve is described as a "model," if we may borrow that word, of the man-woman relationship in the public worship of the congregation. The relationship of Adam and Eve shows and "teaches" what must be characteristic of relationships within the congregation.

With that, however, everything has not yet been said, because as we saw, the historical element is not of essential significance in the notion of a teaching model. The question is whether this last characteristic aspect of the teaching model agrees with what Paul says with reference to Adam and Eve in 1 Timothy 2:13–14. Is the remark of E. F. Scott in his commentary on the Pastoral Letters correct when he says we must keep in mind that while in antiquity it was thought the narrative in Genesis deals with real

25. C. Bouma, *De brieven van den apostel Paulus aan Timotheüs en Titus* (Kampen, 1953), 63, rightly points out that Paul is not thinking here about women ruling over men in general but quite specifically about what happens in gatherings of the congregation. "The instruction bears the character of speaking with authority, of ruling, and that the women may not do."

history, the historical element does not really matter?[26] In our opinion it is impossible to say that. If the historical element in his reference to Adam and Eve in 1 Timothy 2 does not matter for Paul, then his concern is with a "generally valid truth," which then is illustrated by the "narrative" of Adam and Eve.

From which generally valid truth, however, does Paul start then? From the generally valid truth of a natural priority of man over woman (verse 13) and from the generally valid truth of a greater susceptibility to temptation on the part of woman (verse 14)? A. Schlatter, for example, thinks along this line when he says that Paul speaks here of the relative priority of man so far as importance is concerned and of the greater susceptibility of woman to temptation.[27] This also is clearly the view of E. L. Smelik. He says: "But this truth is abiding: the paradise story draws woman's attention to the danger that always threatens her throughout life: she is easily misled and easily misleads.... Sharpness of discernment is not in general her principal quality."[28] About a natural priority of men over women and about a greater susceptibility to temptation on the part of women as generally valid truths, however, we read nothing in Scripture. To confine ourselves only to the latter: Why should women be more susceptible to temptation than men? Is openness to temptation associated more with female than with male character, as Smelik will have us believe? We find nothing like that in Scripture (cf. e.g., Rom. 3:10–18), and it cannot be maintained as a generally valid truth.

26. E. P. Scott, *The Pastoral Epistles* (London, 1948), 27.

27. A. Schlatter, *Die Briefe an die Thessalonicher, Philipper, Timotheus und Titus* (Stuttgart, 1950), 143.

28. E. L. Smelik, *De brieven van Paulus aan Timotheüs, Titus en Filemon* (Nijkerk, 1961), 42.

So, in 1 Timothy 2:13–14 Paul does not start from generally valid truths which Adam and Eve illustrate, but from historical facts.[29] Nothing is said about a generally valid truth of a natural priority of man over woman, but certainly something is said about the fact that Adam was formed first. Just as little is there a generally valid truth of a greater susceptibility to temptation on the part of woman, but certainly there is the fact that Eve fell into temptation first. The facts indeed have at the same time an illustrative significance. If with reference to 1 Timothy 2:13–14, however, one wishes to speak of a "teaching model," it must be clear in any case that in that teaching model the historical element is not a factor to be neglected. In order not to run aground on (nonexistent) general truths, it will be necessary to hold fast to the historical element. The teaching model, if one wishes to persist in speaking of such, does not stand here in a competitive position with regard to history. It is not a matter of either-or but of both-and.

Jude 14

The letter of Jude issues a serious warning directed at false teachers and summons readers to stand fast against these false teachers. In that connection, he mentions Enoch and (quite incidentally) Adam. In verses 14 and 15 Jude says: "It was also about these that Enoch, the seventh from Adam, prophesied, saying, 'Behold, the Lord comes with ten thousands of his holy ones, to execute judgment on all and to convict all the ungodly of all their deeds of ungodliness that they have committed in such an ungodly way, and of all the harsh things that ungodly sinners have spoken against him.'"

29. Cf. Bouma, *De brieven van den apostel Paulus aan Timotheüs en Titus*, 63. See also Ridderbos, *Paul*, 462, who speaks of the "history of the beginning."

Words that practically agree with Jude 14 and 15 are found in one of the apocryphal books, namely, the book of Enoch. It is usually assumed that Jude has borrowed from Enoch at this point.[30] S. Greijdanus, however, denies the use of Enoch by Jude and assumes that these words were preserved in Israel by tradition and so, independently of each other, came to the attention of Jude and the writer of the book of Enoch.[31]

Wherever Jude may have gotten these words, it is clear that for him Enoch is a prophet and, as such, a specific historical figure. When he calls Enoch "the seventh from Adam,"[32] he sees a specific historical distance between Enoch and Adam. The notion of a "teaching model," then, is of no use here. Greijdanus wishes to give this addition a pointed meaning by inserting in thought the words "still only": Enoch, "still only" the seventh from Adam. The meaning, then, would be: When there were still only seven successive generations—Adam reckoned as first—which had been born, the coming of the Lord for judgment was already proclaimed to the ungodly.[33] Probably, however, the information that Enoch is "the seventh from Adam" is a remark made in passing without further significance.[34]

---

30. E.g., J. Moffatt, *The General Epistles. James, Peter and Jude* (London, 1945), 240.

31. S. Greijdanus, *De brieven van de apostelen Petrus en Johannes en de brief van Judas* (Amsterdam, 1929), 636. Cf. also S. Greijdanus, *De brief van Judas* (Kampen, 1950), 115.

32. This characterization also occurs in Enoch 60:8 and 93:3. Cf. also Gen. 5:3–18 and 1 Chron. 1:1–3.

33. Greijdanus, *Petrus, Johannes, Judas*, 637; idem., *Judas*, 115.

34. K. H. Schelkle, *Die Petrusbriefe, Der Judasbrief* (Freiburg-Basel-Wien, 1964), 163, thinks that the number seven is used here as the holy number and the number of God's grace.

4

RABBINIC REFERENCES
TO ADAM

REPEATEDLY the characterization "teaching model" in its application to Adam is connected to references to Adam by the Jewish rabbis. Adam is said to function as a teaching model for the rabbis, and the New Testament references to Adam, especially those of Paul, are allegedly to be seen in the light of the rabbinic references to Adam. Thus, for example, Kuitert says: "Paul deals with the Old Testament as all the Rabbis do.... The Rabbis with whom Paul learned had a flowering theology about Adam and Eve. Without exaggeration, one can say that it was the Rabbis who first began to make use of Adam as a fixture in their theological teaching."[1]

In this connection two questions emerge. The first is whether the writers of the New Testament, among whom we have Paul especially in mind, are really so dependent on rabbinic theology as we are often led to believe. The second question is whether in

---

1. Kuitert, *Do You Understand What You Read?*, 42.

rabbinic theology Adam does as a matter of fact appear as a teaching model in the sense in which this notion is used by Kuitert, that is to say, without concern for the historical element.

Concerning Paul's dependence on rabbinic theology, to limit ourselves simply to him, it is especially noteworthy that there is nothing in rabbinic literature analogous to the parallel between Adam as the first man and Christ as the second (or last) man (1 Cor. 15:45–47). In an interesting article, F. Schiele has emphatically and convincingly maintained that in the rabbinic literature, where it occurs repeatedly, the expression "first Adam" stands by itself. An expression that corresponds to "the last Adam" never occurs in the older rabbinic literature, Schiele concludes. Since the expression "the first Adam" or "Adam, the first" occurs more than a hundred times without an "Adam, the second," or "the last," or "the future" corresponding to it, that can only mean that the expression "Adam, the first" should not at all be understood in contrast with another Adam. Consequently, according to Schiele, for the rabbis the expression "Adam, the first" can only signify the first man in contrast with all subsequent human beings.[2] A treatise in Spanish, dating from the late middle ages, states for the first time that the last man is the Messiah, but this language is certainly dependent upon Christianity.[3] The conclusion that Schiele reaches on the basis of his investigation is that there are no rabbinic parallels to 1 Corinthians 15:45–49, whether according to the letter or the content.[4]

2. F. Schiele, "Die rabbinischen Parallelen zu I Kor. 15, 45–50," *Zeitschrift für wissenschaftliche Theologie* 24 (N.F. 7, 1899): 23–24.

3. Ibid., 29.

4. Ibid., 31.

Strack-Billerbeck came to the same conclusion as Schiele: "Not a trace is to be found . . . of the term 'second' or 'last' man."[5] Likewise unequivocal is the judgment of J. Héring, not only with reference to the rabbinic materials but also to the apocalyptic literature. According to Héring the doctrine of the first and second Adam is to be found neither in Jewish apocalyptic work nor in the Judaism of the Talmud.[6] Thus Paul has not borrowed the parallel of Adam as the first man and Christ as the second man from the Jewish apocalyptic and rabbinic literature which he may have known. Because Paul did not borrow this parallel from other sources either,[7] we must say that Paul himself has introduced the conception of Christ as the last Adam and second man.[8] This one example—and to our way of thinking it is an example central to our topic—shows clearly that direct lines may not be drawn too easily between rabbinic literature and Paul. Naturally, this does not mean a denial of the fact that the rabbinic training that Paul received left a stamp on his person and also on his manner of speaking. In this connection the second question we raised is important, namely, whether in rabbinic

5. Strack-Billerbeck, *Kommentar zum Neuen Testament aus Talmud und Midrasch*, 3, 477–78.

6. J. Héring, *La Première Épître de Saint Paul aux Corinthiens* (Neuchâtel-Paris, 1959), 148.

7. Other sources to be mentioned are: Philo's interpretation of Genesis 1 and 2; the gnostic myth of the primal man; and "Son of Man," as this expression is used in the Gospels as a self-designation of Jesus. It falls outside the scope of this study to show that Paul has not borrowed the parallel "first Adam—last Adam" from one of these sources either. I have tried to provide the proof for that in detail in my dissertation, *Christus en de Geest. Een exegetisch onderzoek naar de verhouding van de opgestane Christus en de Geest van God volgens de brieven van Paulus* (Kampen, 1971).

8. Cf. du Plessis, *Christus as Hoof van Kerk en Kosmos*, 38; W. D. Davies, *Paul and Rabbinic Judaism* (London, 1965), 44; Pop, *De eerste brief van Paulus aan de Corinthiërs*, 393.

literature Adam functions as a teaching model without concern for the historical element.

Here we can first of all tie into what we just saw, that where Adam is called "the first," he is as such distinguished from all other human beings. As "the first," Adam is seen as the one who stands over against all other human beings and precedes them. It is plain that here the qualification "teaching model" is no help at all.

There can be no doubt that in rabbinic literature Adam is spoken of repeatedly as the one in whom what is essential for every human being becomes visible.[9] If the word "model" did not have such a clearly scientific coloration, we would be able here to speak of a "teaching model." The matter that concerns us, however, is whether this significance of Adam stands in a position of competition with his significance as a historical person, or, if it is not a question of competition, in any case still makes his significance as a historical person irrelevant.

There can be no question of that in rabbinic literature. The first thing to be pointed out is that the rabbis also see Adam as the head of the whole of humanity. In this significance Adam occupies a unique position, and it is impossible to put Adam on a line with "man" in general. According to W. D. Davies, on the basis of the unique position of Adam the rabbis reached two conclusions: the unity of the whole of humanity is rooted in Adam and the love commandment is rooted in Adam.[10]

Because Adam is the head and forefather of the whole of humanity, all human beings are one in him and all human beings belong

9. Cf., e.g., Brandenburger, *Adam und Christus. Exegetisch-religionsgeschichtliche Untersuchung zu Römer 5:12–21 (I. Kor. 15)*, 43–44; R. Scroggs, *The Last Adam. A Study in Pauline Anthropology* (London, 1966), 33–34.

10. Davies, *Paul and Rabbinic Judaism*, 53.

to each other. Thus Mischna Sanhedrin 4:5 says: "Therefore but a single man was created in the world to teach that if any man has caused a single soul to perish from Israel, Scripture imputes it to him as though he had caused a whole world to perish, and if any man saves alive a single soul from Israel, Scripture imputes it to him as though he had saved alive a whole world." The love commandment springs directly from this. The unique position of Adam is seen as the basis for the commandment of love, unity, and peace among human beings. Again, reference may be made to Mischna Sanhedrin 4:5: "Again, but a single man was created for the sake of peace among mankind that none should say to his fellow: My father was greater than your father."

These same notions about Adam as the head of humanity are encountered frequently in rabbinic literature from the period directly after the New Testament. It may be assumed that this literature puts into words what was believed earlier. Thus in Pirke Rabbi Eliezer, 11 we read:

The Holy One, blessed be He, spoke to the Torah: "Let us make man in our image, after our likeness" (Gen. 1:26). (The Torah) answered Him: Sovereign of all the worlds . . . , the man whom You will to create will be limited in days and full of anger and he will come under the power of sin. Unless You will be long-suffering with him, it would be well for him not to have come into the world. The Holy One, blessed be He, answered: And is it without reason that I am called "slow to anger" and "abounding in love"? Then He began to collect the dust of the first man from the four corners of the world. . . . Why (did He gather the dust of man) from the four corners of the world? Thus spoke the Holy One, blessed be He: If a man should come from the east to the west or from the west to the east, and his time comes to depart from the world, then the earth shall not say: The dust of your body is not mine, return to the place where you were created. But (this circumstance) teaches you that in every place where a man goes or comes and his end approaches when he must depart from the world, from there is the origin of the dust of his body and there it returns to the dust, as it is said: "For dust you are and unto dust shall you return." (Gen. 3:19)

The thought is that all men are formed from the same dust, because all have come from Adam, who was formed out of dust from the four quarters of the earth.[11] Adam is thus determinative for all men.

This position of Adam as determinative for all men comes out in those texts which state that through Adam sin has come upon all human beings. We find this idea clearly expressed in the apocryphal literature, among which especially 4 Ezra is to be mentioned. In 4 Ezra 4:30 the sin of Adam is seen as a seed from which the harvest of all other godlessness has come. "For a grain of evil seed was sown in the heart of Adam from the beginning, and how much fruit of godlessness has it produced up to this time, and shall yet produce until the harvest comes." We find this idea still more clearly in chapter 7:

And I [Ezra] answered and said: This is my first and last word; better had it been that the earth had not produced Adam, or else, having once produced him (for you) to have restrained him from sinning. For how does it profit us all that in the present we

11. For examples that make clear how strictly physical this was understood for the most part, see Davies, *Paul and Rabbinic Judaism*, 54–55.

must live in grief and after death look for punishment? O Adam, what have you done! For though it was you who sinned, the fall was not yours alone, but ours also who are your descendants! (4 Ezra 7:116–118, according to another enumeration: 46–48).

According to Brandenburger these words do not express the intention of the author of 4 Ezra himself.[12] Even if that is correct, in any case it is evident from these words that the ideas that come to expression in them were alive at the time 4 Ezra was written.[13] Adam is clearly thought of as someone whose position was determinative for all his descendants.

Ellis also uncovers this in rabbinic literature, where he points to the rabbinic doctrine of "the evil impulse." According to the rabbis two impulses are always struggling against each other in man: the good and the evil impulse. In the rabbinic literature, in the opinion of Ellis, the evil impulse is due to the sin of Adam.[14] However, the question to be raised here with Brandenburger is whether the "evil impulse" really is to be taken back to the sin of Adam or by it something is meant which is present in man as such.[15]

In rabbinic literature, the determinative position of Adam for all men with reference to death comes out clearly. It is through Adam and through the sin of Adam that death has come upon man. This is expressed clearly by Rabbi Jehuda (ca. AD 150): "You are children of the first man who has brought death upon

12. Brandenburger, *Adam und Christus. Exegetisch-religionsgeschichtliche Untersuchung zu Römer 5:12–21 (I. Kor. 15)*, 30ff.

13. Cf. ibid., 36. In this connection see also the Apocalypse of Baruch 17:3; 23:4; 48:42ff; 45:15, 19.

14. Ellis, *Paul's Use of the Old Testament*, 59.

15. Cf. Brandenburger, *Adam und Christus. Exegetisch-religionsgeschichtliche Untersuchung zu Römer 5:12–21 (I. Kor. 15)*, 43.

you as a punishment, as well as upon all his descendants who come after him until the end of all generations."[16] The same rabbi also says, "Only one commandment, a prohibition, was given to Adam and he transgressed it. See! How many deaths have followed as a result upon him and his generations and the generations of his generations until the end of his generations."[17]

The expression "death came upon him [Adam] and upon his descendants" is almost a stereotype in rabbinic literature.[18] Although we encounter this notion especially in literature that dates from the time after the New Testament, we may assume that it was current before it was put into words. The fact that death is repeatedly characterized as punishment for individual sin[19] is not in conflict with the unique position of Adam with reference to death. The one is true as well as the other.

In conclusion we can say that the rabbinic literature clearly refers to the unique position of Adam. That uniqueness is evident from the fact that in different respects Adam is determinative for those who are his descendants. Justice is not done to this unique position, if an effort is made to characterize all the references to Adam in rabbinic literature by the concept "teaching model."

---

16. Sifre Deut. 32:32

17. Sifra Lev. 5:17.

18. Brandenburger, *Adam und Christus. Exegetisch-religionsgeschichtliche Untersuchung zu Römer 5:12–21 (I. Kor. 15)*, 60.

19. Cf. Strack-Billerbeck, *Kommentar zum Neuen Testament aus Talmud und Midrasch*, 3:228–29.

5

A DISTANCE BETWEEN INTENTION AND SIGNIFICANCE?

IT IS ASSUMED for the most part, then, that Paul did view Adam as a historical person and not merely as a "model" of man in general, although it is added in the same breath that today we no longer are nor can be bound to this view of Paul.

As an example of this position we can refer to Alan Richardson. For Richardson, too, it is an established fact that today we can no longer think of Adam as a historical person. For us Adam has significance only as an idea, that is to say, a theological symbol. For us he represents the unity and the solidarity of the human race, as it is created in God's image, rebels against God, and at the same time remains the object of the love of God. Nevertheless Richardson can state with the greatest certainty that Paul "undoubtedly" thought of Adam as a historical individual.[1]

1. A. Richardson, *An Introduction to the Theology of the New Testament* (London, 1961), 248.

Thus a clear distance emerges between what Paul intended to say in his day and what his words mean for us today. Kuitert does not go so far. He thinks that he is able in his view of Adam to agree with Paul's real intention. According to Kuitert, Paul did not *wish* to provide in Adam anything other than a teaching model, whereby the historical element was of quite subordinate significance, or even was to be neglected entirely.[2] Kuitert certainly does not want to disregard the intended meaning of Paul but wants to do justice to it. However, he is wrong in thinking that he is able to agree with Paul's real intention, because, as we have seen, the historical element in Adam is much more important for Paul than Kuitert will have us believe. Thus for Kuitert, too, there is *in fact* a distance between Paul's intention when he refers to Adam and the significance of those references for us today.

Now with this distance between intention and significance *taken by itself* certainly everything has not yet been said. It is difficult to deny that the biblical writers have in many respects rendered the revelation of God with the help of conceptions that possessed general validity in their own time but which by now have lost their validity. Not unjustly in this connection, reference is repeatedly made to the case of Galileo.[3] Following Copernicus, Galileo maintained that the sun does not revolve around the earth, as was generally assumed at that time, but that, conversely, the earth revolves around the sun. It is clear from Scripture that also in the time of the biblical writers it was held that the sun revolves around the earth (cf. especially Joshua 10:12–13). On the basis

2. Kuitert, *Do You Understand What You Read?*, 40.
3. Cf., e.g., G. C. Berkouwer, *De Heilige Schrift* (Kampen, 1967), 2:92; Kuitert, *Do You Understand What You Read?*, 37ff.

of Scripture, Galileo was condemned by a decree of the Holy Office in 1616. This condemnation (which later naturally lost its significance entirely) did not in any way reckon with the fact that the biblical writers could only express the place of the earth in the universe in accordance with the knowledge they possessed at that time and not in accordance with the knowledge that would only be obtained centuries later.

In this connection Berkouwer speaks of the "level of knowledge" of the biblical writers in a particular time. By that he means that the biblical writers did not put into words "timeless" truths but wrote in a particular language they understood, with a style that was their own, and also with conceptions that agreed with what they knew.[4] As a matter of fact the biblical writers—we should almost say: naturally—could only write about questions such as the place of the earth in the universe in accordance with the insights they possessed.

The question at issue here, however, is whether the way in which Paul and the entire New Testament speak about Adam can be viewed as a way of speaking in which only a particular "level of knowledge" comes to expression. Is what Scripture says about Adam (in this respect) on the same level with what it says about the place of the earth in the universe?[5] If that would be the case, the intention of the biblical writers could certainly be to speak about Adam as the first historical person and head of humanity, but we would no longer be bound to that intention (since it belongs to a particular "level of knowledge"), and the significance for us

4. Berkouwer, *De Heilige Schrift*, 2:93.
5. Emphatic on this point is J. Lever, *Waar blijven we?* (Kampen-Wageningen, 1969), 19–24.

of these references to Adam would be divorced from the meaning they originally possessed.

In order to be able to answer this question we would have to pay attention to the contexts in which Adam is discussed. Decisive is the fact, as we saw, that in a specific way Adam is on a par with Christ. This does not mean that Christ and his work are anchored in Adam, as Kuitert rightly says. However, it is also not right if one says, as Kuitert does, that Adam only illumines Christ and his work in its meaning and purpose.[6] Following Ridderbos, we established that the fact that Adam is a type of Christ (Rom. 5:14) indicates that a redemptive-historical correlation exists between Adam and Christ. With reference both to Adam and to Christ it is a matter of a structure ordained by God, namely, the structure of the "all through one." What held with reference to Adam holds completely with reference to Christ. Adam is not only an illustration of Christ. Christ is the fulfillment of Adam.

Therefore, if in the case of Adam the intention of Paul in his own time is divorced from its significance for us today, that must also have consequences with respect to Christ. For the redemptive-historical correlation between Adam and Christ entails that if what Paul says about Adam no longer holds for us, it is impossible to see why what he says about Christ *in the same context* must still hold for us. What is the sense of an antitype, if there is no type? What is the sense of a fulfillment, if there is nothing to fulfill? The redemptive-historical correlation that Paul sees between Adam and Christ means that no longer honoring Paul's intention when he speaks about Adam must entail no longer honoring Paul's intention when he speaks about Christ. For these two are—in

6. Kuitert, *Do You Understand What You Read?*, 40.

their redemptive-historical correlation—related to *each other.* To no longer honor Paul's intention when he speaks about Adam entails that the framework in which Paul places Christ and his work, collapses.

There are many who see no difficulty, not only with reference to Adam but also with reference to Christ, in radically divorcing the intention of Paul's words from their significance for us. This comes out most pointedly in connection with the typology of Adam and Christ in 1 Corinthians 15, when Adam, as the one in whom "all" die, is contrasted with the resurrected Christ, in whom "all" will be made alive.

It is clear that the *intention* of Paul in 1 Corinthians 15 is to speak about the resurrection of Christ as a historical fact in the sense of an event that took place at a datable time and in a demonstrable place.[7] Paul appeals to the resurrection of Christ as part of the legitimizing of his apostleship (1 Cor. 15:8–9). If the legitimizing of Paul and the other apostles did not have a historical fact for its basis, then it has no basis at all, and as a legitimizing it was utterly deficient.[8] Certainly at stake in this matter was not only the reality of the appearances of Christ but the reality of the resurrection as well.[9]

W. Marxsen especially, however, in no way considers himself bound to this clear intent of the apostolic witness concerning the

7. Cf. J. N. Sevenster, *Leven en dood in de brieven van Paulus* (Amsterdam, 1954), 103; D. P. Fuller, *Easter Faith and History* (Grand Rapids, 1965), 253ff.; K. H. Rengstorf, *Die Auferstehung Jesu. Form, Art und Sinn der urchristlichen Osterbotschaft* (Witten/Ruhr, 1967), 105ff.

8. Cf. esp. U. Wilckens, "Der Ursprung der Uberlieferung der Erscheinungen des Auferstandenen. Zur traditionsgeschichtliche Analyse von I Kor 15, 1–11," *Dogma und Denkstrukturen*, ed. W. Joest and W. Pannenberg (Göttingen, 1963), 81.

9. Cf. Rengstorf, *Die Auferstehung Jesu*, 62.

resurrection.[10] According to Marxsen, at that time people lived in the firm conviction that Christ had risen from the grave, and on the basis of this conviction Paul spoke about the resurrection of Christ in 1 Corinthians 15, but we are no longer able to share that conviction and may no longer speak in that way. The disciples really "saw" something following the death of Jesus (1 Cor. 15:5–8) and on the basis of that "seeing" drew the conclusion of the resurrection. Thus the resurrection was not a real event but a human conclusion. In this connection Marxsen speaks of an "Interpretament," that is, an attempt at interpretation. Therefore he can also say: "Today it is no longer possible for us to speak directly about the resurrection of Jesus as a real event. We simply have to say that it is a matter of an effort at interpretation which was employed by those who (at that time!) reflected upon their experience of "'seeing.'"[11] If we would want to connect the resurrection with a particular historical event, we would be guilty of a forbidden historicizing, even though in an earlier time that historicizing was understandable and perhaps even necessary.

We shall have to reject a view like that of Marxsen. When he divorces the intended meaning of Paul's words from their significance for us, then the apostolic message is affected at its core.[12] Apart from the resurrection of Christ, understood according to the *intention* of Paul, faith is futile, believers are still in their sins, and those who have fallen asleep in Christ are lost (1 Cor. 15:17–18).

10. W. Marxsen, "Die Auferstehung Jesu als historisches und als theologisches Problem," in *Die Bedeutung der Auferstehungsbotschaft für den Glauben an Jesus Christus* (Gütersloh, 1966), 9–39. W. Marxsen, *Die Auferstehung Jesu von Nazareth* (Gütersloh, 1968).

11. Marxsen, *Auferstehungsbotschaft*, 23.

12. Cf. also Berkouwer, *H. Schrift*, 2:232.

If we reject a view such as Marxsen's, however, we have to real-
ize that in 1 Corinthians 15 the resurrection of Christ is discussed
in a particular framework: the framework of the redemptive-
historical correlation between Adam and Christ. What became
historical reality in the resurrection of Christ is the antitypical
fulfillment of what became historical reality in the fall of Adam
into sin. If we wish to speak about the resurrection of Christ
according to the *intention* of Paul, we will have to let that resurrection stand in the same framework in which it was put by Paul.
If we do not do that, the question of J. Kamphuis is to the point:
"But *if* it is true that in this argumentation we are dealing with
the disciple of the rabbis, who used Adam as an 'instructional
model' or a 'teaching model,' while he was not really interested in
his historical existence, then the question will never allow itself to
be definitively suppressed: Is not Christ in his resurrection also a
'teaching model' in this dogmatic argumentation, or if one wills,
in this preaching and in this witness?" To that Kamphuis adds a
second question: "And suppose that Paul . . . did indeed believe in
the historicity of the first Adam but that this is no longer relevant
for us . . . , because we are only interested in the function of Adam
as a 'teaching model,' why should we . . . not take the same view
regarding the last Adam?"[13]

From the contexts in which Adam is discussed it is apparent
that we cannot dispose of the question of the historical existence
of Adam with a reference to Paul's "level of knowledge." Discussion of Adam is not of the same order as, for instance, discussion
of the place of the earth in the universe! For Paul it is too clearly
a matter of identical structures for Adam and Christ. Christ

---

13. J. Kamphuis, "Verstaat gij wat gij leest? IV," *De Reformatie* 44 (1969): 148.

and his work come to stand in an entirely different light, if the structure that holds for him and for Adam is not the same and if we can no longer speak of a redemptive-historical correlation between Adam and Christ. Justice can only be done to the "as in Adam . . . so in Christ" of 1 Corinthians 15:22, if we continue to speak of a redemptive-historical correlation between Adam and Christ and if we continue to see Adam as the representative head of humanity, who no less than Christ occupied a specific place in (redemptive) *history*.

6

CONSEQUENCES

THE PRECEDING discussion should have made clear that a great deal is at stake in the questions concerning Adam as a historical person or teaching model (if an antithesis is made of these two!). Therefore it is simply not true when Kuitert says: "It is not Adam, not a theory about the Bible, but the message of Jesus Christ that makes Christians of men. This is why faith is not changed if Adam is shown not to have been a historical person. The reality of Jesus is not built upon what the Bible says about Adam. The reality of Jesus stands by itself."[1] Naturally it is true that "the message of Jesus Christ" makes men Christians. The difficulty arises, however, when Kuitert follows this up with the words "this is why."

Is it really so that because "the message of Jesus Christ" makes Christians Christians, faith is not changed if Adam is shown not to have been a historical person? J. T. Bakker rightly says that this conclusion is "hardly evident." With no less right he adds: "That there are so many who are still not able to dispense with Adam

1. Kuitert, *Do You Understand What You Read?*, 40.

61

is not explained by their fundamentalism or by their attachment to an interpretation of the past but by the fact that the 'one after the other' of creation and fall is something other than the 'next to each other' of creation and sin."[2]

If in antithesis to Adam as a historical person, Adam is to be spoken of as a teaching model, that in fact involves *a particular view of sin*. If Adam only lets us see what is characteristic of *everyone*, because Adam is man in general so that the sin of Adam is also the sin of man in general, and if on the other hand Adam may no longer be regarded as the one man through whom sin has come into the world, it is apparent that in a certain sense sin belongs to man as such. Sin has thus become a given "next to" creation. Consequently, in Romans 5:12 Paul does not say how sin invaded creation but only that there is sin and that sin is always an affair of man. With Bakker, however, one has to say that it makes a good deal of difference whether in Romans 5 Paul expresses himself in terms of a historical framework that does service as clothing for the supratemporal truth that the good creation is from God and sin an affair of ours, or in Romans 5 Paul intends rather to say how sin has invaded the good creation of God.[3] The concept "teaching model" cannot do justice to the latter. If Adam were only a teaching model, he would only be an illustration of man in whom sin is inherent. The concept "teaching model" eliminates the "one after the other" of creation and fall, and only leaves room for the "next to each other" of creation and sin.

In essence, then, one may no longer speak of the *guilt* of sin. This becomes clear in a striking manner in *The New Catechism*. We have seen that the writers of this "declaration of the faith for

---

2. J. T. Bakker, "Verstaat gij wat gij leest?," *Gereformeerd Weekblad* 24 (1969): 251.
3. Ibid.

adults" want to know nothing of a historical Adam. The echo of the word "one" in Romans 5 is merely a literary form, and we are assured that we need "not attach special significance to a 'first sin.'" This view of Adam appears to have direct consequences for the *Catechism's* view of sin. In the same context in which the existence of Adam as a historical person is denied we read that it is not to be said "per se that all sins could be entirely avoided." Even clearer is the remark that follows: ". . . that evil occurs is perhaps practically unavoidable."[4] Where evil thus becomes a "practically unavoidable" matter, sin loses its character of guilt. It is worth noting that nowhere in the index of *The New Catechism* is there a separate listing of the places where the word "guilt" is used. Behind the word "guilt" in the index on page 599 is the entry, "see 'sin.'"

Since *The New Catechism* makes no mention of a first man through whom sin entered the world, a place is given to sin within the process of evolution as a whole. The origin of sin has "something to do" with human freedom. "In humanity freedom grew and with it, sin." "In a world in the process of growing up," sin consists in "a denial of growth toward what conscience shows us."[5] In this way, as W. H. Velema has said, sin becomes an "almost unavoidable growth disturbance in the process of evolution."[6]

Similar ideas are found in the booklet *Waar blijven we?* by J. Lever. He, too, will not recognize Adam as a first historical man. In a process of evolution God has made man to originate from the highest living organisms.[7] Adam is seen as a teaching

4. *De nieuwe katechismus*, 309–10.
5. Ibid., 310–11.
6. W. H. Velema, "God en mens," *Interview met de nieuwe katechismus* (Amsterdam, 1967), 13.
7. Lever, *Waar blijven we?*, 44.

model, when Lever says that in Adam it is a matter of "the deepest problems of every man, of all men, beginning with the first man." For Lever, too, this leads to the idea of the "next to each other" of creation and sin. He says, "Always since the very beginning man has stood over against God in the tension between good and evil, and evil has affected his life. Throughout the whole of history man has always made the evil choice."[8] If evil is so interwoven with human existence, it is difficult to maintain the character of sin as guilt. That is also said in so many words by Lever when he asserts: "Presumably therefore our species has always been marked by the use of weapons. Our bodies are so vulnerable and so lacking in means of defense like claws and fangs and we are so carnivorous by origin that we can only hold our own by means of clubs, bones and stone objects. In fights between members of our species blows that are too hard quickly result."[9] It is difficult to conclude anything else from this than that man—given the vulnerability of his body—must always be as he has been down to the present.

It should be clear that by speaking of Adam as a teaching model in opposition to Adam as a historical person, faith is left anything but undisturbed. Where the teaching model takes the place of the historical person, the "next to each other" of creation and sin replaces the "one after the other" of creation and fall, and correspondingly alters one's view of the character of sin.

In the second place, referring to Adam as a teaching model in antithesis to Adam as a historical person involves *a particular view of redemption.* As we have seen, in Romans 5:12–21 Paul contrasts

8..Ibid., 28.
9. Ibid., 61.

the redeeming work of Christ as the one act of obedience with the sin of Adam as the one act of disobedience. Now in Romans 5, all sorts of words are used for the sin of Adam which indicate clearly the guilty character of that sin. The sin of Adam was a "trespass" and a "disobedience." The redeeming work of Christ, which stands in opposition to this sin of Adam, therefore bears the character of *atonement for guilt.*

If Adam may no longer be viewed as a historical person but in him is revealed only what is inherent in every man, so that, as we just saw, one can hardly still talk about guilt in the proper sense of the word, then the character of redemption also naturally changes. That becomes clear once again in a striking manner in *The New Catechism.* Here redemption is on a par with "progress."[10] The atoning character of Christ's work of redemption recedes sharply into the background. Jesus' blood, so *The New Catechism* says, is "not so much a gift to God but from God. Jesus does not give his blood to a Father who demands punishment but to us."[11] In this "not (so much) . . . but," oppositions are created that are not present in Scripture.[12] These antitheses are bound up with a view of the character of sin, and the way in which one evaluates the references in Scripture to Adam is anything but irrelevant to that view.

In direct connection with the preceding is the fact that to speak about Adam as a teaching model in antithesis to Adam as a historical person involves *a particular view of the Redeemer.* We recall again the warning that Bultmann sounded in the direction

10. *De nieuwe katechismus,* 328.
11. Ibid., 331.
12. Cf., e.g., Mark 10:45; 1 Cor. 6:20; Heb. 9:22.

of Barth: If the figure of Adam becomes an idea, Christ, too, threatens to become an idea. If the significance of Adam consists entirely in the fact that he is the image of man in his sinfulness and disobedience before God, it is only one step further to maintaining that the significance of Christ likewise consists entirely in the fact that he is the image of man as God intends him to be and as he someday will be. It can no longer be an occasion for surprise that once again we encounter this idea in *The New Catechism*. The significance of Christ is stated in these words: "There *is* a good man in the world."[13] Therefore the history of the church can also be characterized as "general humanization since Christ."[14] Christ's significance as Redeemer lies particularly in His humanity, because His humanity provides the guarantee of progress and the completion of the process of evolution. We also meet with corresponding ideas in Hendrikus Berkhof. It is Christ who raises humanity "to a higher level for which the children of Adam are ultimately destined." In this connection, according to Berkhof, the thought intrudes "that this outlook finds its analogy in modern insights into evolution: again and again there is an individual within a species who metamorphoses to a higher form of existence, whereby life is laid open to new possibilities. Is Jesus Christ the name for the turn whereby evolution finds its crowning and God's creation reaches its ultimate destiny?" It should be said here that Berkhof "hastily" breaks off this train of thought, because he is aware that it leads him "up to and over the edge of a Christian metaphysics."[15]

13. *De nieuwe katechismus*, 332.
14. Ibid., 273.
15. H. Berkhof, *De mens onderweg* ('s-Gravenhage, 1960), 95–96.

If an evolutionary view leaves no place for Adam as a historical person and has a place for Adam only as a teaching model, that has direct consequences so far as its view of Christ is concerned. That became particularly evident to us in *The New Catechism*. Christ as Redeemer is also thought of within the whole of an evolutionary framework. The humanity of Christ receives all the emphasis, while the preaching of Scripture that Christ is not only man but also in a unique sense the Son of God recedes into the background.

To be occupied with the question of how Scripture speaks about Adam is thus anything but an insignificant problem of detail. As the first historical man and head of humanity, Adam is not mentioned merely in passing in the New Testament. The redemptive-historical correlation between Adam and Christ determines the framework in which—particularly for Paul—the redemptive work of Christ has its place. That work of redemption can no longer be confessed according to the meaning of Scripture, if it is divorced from the framework in which it stands there. Whoever divorces the work of redemption from the framework in which it stands in Scripture no longer allows the Word to function as the norm that determines *everything*. There has been no temptation through the centuries to which theology has been more exposed than this temptation. There is no danger that theology has more to fear than this danger.